Bobryshev Denys

Addressables in Unity

pocket guide

2024

Every developer faces questions about reducing build size, how to load resources and unload unnecessary ones. At the time of writing, using Addressables will solve these questions. The book was created as a note for different situations. And should help from start loading to dynamically loaded resources, as well as unloading resources that are no longer in use.

Content

4

6

About the Author

I'm a regular Unity programmer, at the time of writing I'm on support for an old game of the city builder genre. Before me there were many programmers on the project and everyone left their mark. And here I was left on the project alone on support. The game was already close to 150 mb, and had to think sometimes before production, because at the moment on android there is a limit and above did not pass. The project was already set up to load AssetBundles with events and part of the graphics through Addressables. But, somehow came the task to reduce the build to 100 mb. Literally recently searched for where 1-2 mb to throw out of the build, and here 50 mb. It made me break the main rule - if it works - do not touch. The game is quite large and part of the content needed by the player, part of the player has but not needed, there are temporary resources. But we will not talk about my work, this is just the trigger that forced to delve into Addressables. At the moment there is not enough information. There are courses, forums. And I started to take notes for myself, which I want to share with you in this book

Preface

I'd like to point out that the main purpose of this book is to introduce you to loading resources into your project using Addressablas as an example. So we won't cover basic things like how to create a project and the Unity3d interface - if you don't already know that, it's too early for you to consider this book. We're also not going to build a game, we're not going to look at architectural issues - there are other books, courses, materials for that. I apologise in advance for the beauty of the code - every team has its own case, as well as approaches, and the essence of the book is primarily to help with loading resources using Addressablass.

Introduction

So let's get started. We have a project, be it a game or an application, the result of which is most likely a build for a mobile device. And although mobile devices are not weak and not very limited in memory, it is still worthwhile to make the application itself as small as possible. Therefore, you need to take out of the build everything that you can, or everything that will come out. If you have a small project and you can take out at once scenes - it's one task and when loading the game - you pump out all the necessary and so until the next update or changes in resources. But there are larger projects, when you do not need to pump out everything, or do not need it for each player, because someone has a low level, someone does not have this building, this weapon, etc. And there is no reason for a player to pump out resources that he does not see in the game at the moment. In such cases, you should load only the most necessary things at the start and load the rest as needed.

What are **AssetBundles** and why do I need them?

AssetBundles are special containers for storing assets (resources) that can be loaded at runtime in Unity applications. They allow developers to load resources as needed, rather than having them all in memory at once. **AssetBundles** allow you to create applications with dynamic content updates and optimise memory usage, which is especially useful for games with a lot of graphics and multimedia resources.

The main advantages of using **AssetBundles:**

1. **Memory saving:** With AssetBundles, you can load only those resources that are needed at a given moment. For example, if a game has many levels, the resources for each level can be loaded and unloaded as needed without taking up extra memory.

2. **Dynamic content updates**: AssetBundles allow you to update content without having to release a new version of the application. For example, you can add new character skins, textures, models or levels that will be downloaded to the user on the next launch or even in real time.

3. **Download flexibility: AssetBundles** support a variety of download formats: they can be downloaded from the device's local storage as well as from the network. This is useful for apps that require regular content updates or want to adjust to user preferences.

4. **Smaller build size:** Instead of including all resources at once in an application build, you can use **AssetBundles** to reduce the size of the application's download package, which improves the initial download and installation speed.

AssetBundles usage scenarios:

Example 1. Loading levels: Let's say you have a game with multiple levels, each using unique textures, models, and sounds. You can create separate AssetBundles for each level. When the player reaches a new level, the game loads only the assets it needs, and unloads them from memory when finished.

Example 2. Customisation and skins: For games with characters and their customisation (e.g. selection of skins, weapons, items), you can create separate **AssetBundles** for each set. This way, players can load only the skins and items they have chosen, not all possible combinations.

Example 3. Real-time content: Many applications use **AssetBundles** to update content on the fly. For example, in learning apps, you can upload lessons or presentations without having to update the entire app in the shop. This can also be useful in news apps where data needs to be constantly updated.

What are **Addressables?**

Addressablas (Addressable Asset System) is a powerful asset management tool in Unity that allows you to simplify the process of loading and unloading assets in your project. **Addressables** allow developers to identify and load assets by their 'addresses' without worrying about where and how those assets are stored in the final build of the game. The system supports working with local and remote resources, allowing the content of a game to be dynamically updated even after its release. This is especially useful for mobile games and applications where it is important to minimise the amount of downloaded data and efficiently manage downloads from servers.

Why use **Addressables?**

As a project grows and the number of assets increases, there is a need to optimise the handling of resources. The benefits of **Addressables** become apparent in the following cases:

Optimised memory usage: resources are loaded only when they are needed and can be unloaded to free up memory.

Asynchronous loading: allows resources to be loaded in the background without blocking the main game thread, improving performance.

Flexibility and scalability: Addressables make it easy to manage resources on both local devices and remote servers, making it easy to release updates and patches to the game.

Simplify development: using Addressables reduces the need for complex manipulation of AssetBundles, making the process intuitive and more automated.

1. **Optimised memory usage:** resources are loaded only when they are needed and can be unloaded to free up memory.

2. **Asynchronous loading:** allows resources to be loaded in the background without blocking the main game thread, improving performance.

3. **Flexibility and scalability:** Addressables make it easy to manage resources on both local devices and remote servers, making it easy to release updates and patches to the game.

4. **Simplify development:** using Addressables reduces the need for complex manipulation of AssetBundles, making the process intuitive and more automated.

Example of using **Addressables**

Let's consider a simple example. Suppose you need to upload an image or 3D model only when the user requests it. With **Addressables**, this is done in a few steps:

1. You assign a unique address to the resource.

2. In the code, call for it to be loaded at that address.

3. Asynchronously load the resource and display it in the game.

This approach allows you not to load all resources at once, which is especially useful in large games with a lot of content.

Section 1: Installing and Configuring Addressables

1.1 How do I add Addressables to a Unity project?

Addressables is a package that can be added through the Unity Package Manager. Follow these steps to install Addressables in your project:

1. **Opening Unity and loading a project**
   Start Unity and open the project in which you want to use Addressables. If you don't have a project yet, create a new one via Unity Hub.

2. **Opening Package Manager**
   From the top menu of Unity, select *Window > Package Manager*. This will open the Package Manager window where you can manage the packages installed in the project.

3. **Searching for Addressables**
   In the Package Manager window, make sure the **Unity Registry** source is selected. In the search bar, type **Addressables**.

4. **Installing a package**
   Select the Addressables package from the list and click **Install**. Unity will automatically install the required dependencies and add the necessary files to the project.

5. **Initialising Addressables**
   After installing the package, you need to initialise Addressables in the project. To do this, go to *Window > Asset Management > Addressables > Groups*. This will open the Addressables Groups window where the basic structure for asset management will be created.

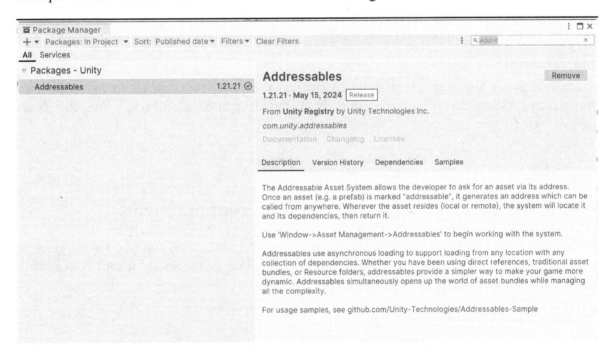

1.2 Creating Addressable Groups

Addressable Groups are logical groups of resources that allow you to manage the building and loading of resources more efficiently. Creating and properly organising groups helps optimise memory usage and load times.

Steps for creating **Addressable Groups:**

1. **Opening the Addressables Groups window**
   If the Addressables Groups window is not already open, go to *Window > Asset Management > Addressables > Groups.*

2. **Create a new group**
   In the Addressables Groups window, click the + (plus) button at the top of the window and select a group type. The most commonly used group types are:
   > **Default Local Group:** for resources stored locally in the project.
   > **Remote Group:** for resources stored on a remote server.
   > **Packed Assets Group:** for resources packaged together.

3. **Configuring a group**
   After creating a group, you can configure its settings:
   > **Bundled Assets:** indicate that the resources will be packaged into **AssetBundles.**
   > **Build Path:** the path where the assembled **AssetBundles** will be stored.
   > **Load Path:** the path from where **AssetBundles** will be loaded at runtime.

For example, you can leave the default settings for the local group and set the remote server URL for the remote group.

Adding resources to a group
To add resources to a group, drag them from the **Project Window** to the desired group in the Addressables Groups window. Alternatively, you can select the resource, right-click and select *Simplify Addressables > Move to New Group*.

1.3 Basic configuration of profiles for different platforms

Addressables profiles allow you to create different build configurations for different platforms or environments (e.g. development, testing, production). This is especially useful if you want to use different resource loading paths depending on the environment.

Create and configure profiles:

1. **Opening the Profiles window**
   In the Addressables Groups window, click the **Profile** button (usually a gear icon) and select **Manage Profiles.**

2. **Create a new profile**
   In the Manage Profiles window, click the **Add** button and enter a name for the new profile, such as **Development** or **Production**.

3. **Configuring profile variables**
   Each profile contains a set of variables that define paths and settings for Addressables. The main variables are:

   - **LocalBuildPath**: the path for the local build of AssetBundles.
   - **RemoteBuildPath**: the path for a remote build of AssetBundles.
   - **LocalLoadPath**: path to load AssetBundles locally at runtime.
   - **RemoteLoadPath**: the path to remotely load AssetBundles at runtime.

   Customise these paths according to your needs. For example, you can use local paths for the **Development** profile and remote servers for **Production**.

4. **Applying a profile to groups**
   Once you have created and configured the profiles, you need to assign them to the appropriate groups:

   - Select the desired group in the **Addressables Groups** window.
   - In the **Inspector**, find the **Build** and **Load Path settings**.
   - Use the profile variables to specify the appropriate paths. For example, instead of a hard-coded path, use *${LocalBuildPath}*.

5. **Switching between profiles**
   To switch between profiles (for example, from **Development** to **Production**), open the **Profiles** window and select the desired profile from the list. This will automatically update the paths and settings for all groups that use variables from that profile.

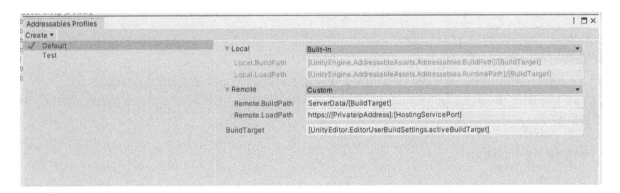

1.4. Addressables Assets Settings: basic settings and recommendations

1. Build and Load Paths

- **Build Path**: Specifies where the collected Addressables data will be located on your local machine.
- **Load Path**: Determines where the application will load AssetBundles from in the runtime.

Recommendations:

- In most cases, Build Path is set to the StreamingAssets folder so that resources are available both during development and after the project is built.
- **Load Path** is usually installed on a server or cloud storage so that resources can be loaded dynamically. For local testing you can also use **StreamingAssets**.

2. Catalog Settings

- **Player Version Override**: Allows you to manually set the catalogue version. This is useful for managing content versions and compatibility.
- **Compress Catalog**: An option that compresses a directory to reduce its size and speed up loading times.

Recommendations:

- Use Compress Catalog to reduce download time, especially on a slow internet connection.
- The Player Version Override option comes in handy if you are updating content on the server but want to maintain compatibility with a specific version of the application.

3. Build and Play Mode Scripts

- **Build Script**: Defines the build process for Addressables. The main **BuildScriptPackedMode** script is responsible for creating **AssetBundles** for different platforms.
- **Play Mode Script: Allows you to select a mode for testing resources in the editor. Available options:**
    - **Use Asset Database** (fast loading from Unity database, used for testing without creating AssetBundles).
    - **Simulate Groups** (simulate working with AssetBundles without creating them).
    - **Use Existing Build** (uses already built AssetBundles).

Recommendations:

- **Use Use Asset Database** for rapid development - this allows you to test changes quickly.
- For more realistic testing, use Simulate Groups or Use Existing Build to see the behaviour when working with real AssetBundles.

4. Content Update Restrictions

- Allows you to manage the upgrade of individual resources, avoiding re-building all Addressables.

Recommendations:

- Separate frequently updated resources into separate **Addressables** groups to minimise the need for a complete rebuild.
- This setting comes in handy for apps with regular updates, as it allows you to update content more accurately and cost-effectively

5. Advanced Settings

- **Log Runtime Exceptions:** Allows **Addressables** errors to be output to the console at runtime.
- **Unique Bundle IDs:** Includes unique IDs for each **AssetBundle** to help avoid caching issues on the device.

- **Contiguous Bundles:** Option to provide faster sequential loading of resources by bundling them into a single **AssetBundle.**
- **Build Remote Catalog:** Creates a remote catalogue that can be updated without having to reinstall the application. This is useful for applications with large amounts of content and frequent updates.

Recommendations:

- **Log Runtime Exceptions** are recommended to be enabled during development for debugging, but disabled in the release version to avoid unnecessary information in the logs.
- **Unique Bundle IDs** should preferably be left enabled to ensure that assert updates are always loaded correctly, without cache conflicts.
- **Contiguous Bundles** are useful if you have large groups of related resources that are loaded together.
- **Build Remote Catalog** is ideal for projects that frequently update content. In this case, the resource catalogue can be updated on the server without recompiling the application.

6. Groups Settings

Allows you to create and customise groups for assets. Each group can be given unique settings:
- **Packing Mode**: A way to package assets in AssetBundles.
- **Bundle Naming Mode**: AssetBundles naming convention.
- **Addressables Group Schema**: Allows you to specify additional parameters for the group (e.g., how to load, cache, update).

Recommendations:

- Divide assets into groups depending on their use (e.g. UI, levels, sounds). This allows you to efficiently manage resource loading and unloading.
- Use **Pack Separately** mode for resources that can be loaded and unloaded independently.
- Customise **Bundle Naming Mode** depending on your project structure and caching requirements.

1.5. Adressables

You can add a resource to **Addressables** in two ways:

1. From the **Project** window, drag and drop the object into the desired group

2. At the selected object in the **Inspector** window there is a tick **Addressable** - which throws to the group by default, and further you need to move to the desired group.

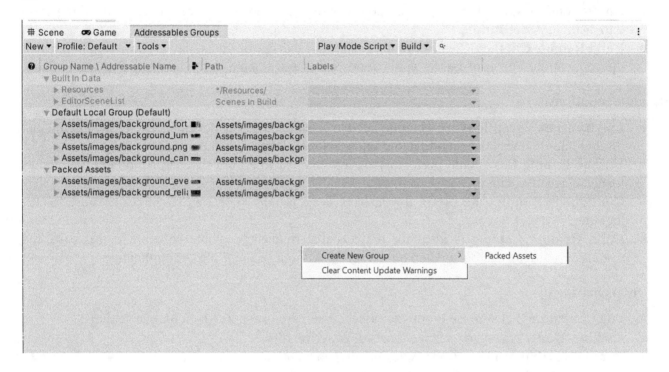

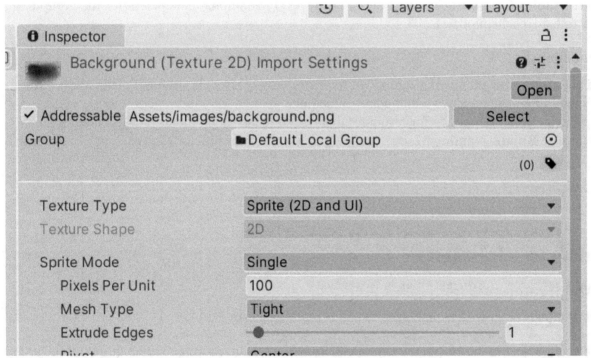

After installing and configuring **Addressables**, it's important to make sure everything is working correctly.

1. **Addressables assembly**
   In the Addressables Groups window, click on the **Build** button and select *New Build > Default Build Script*. This will start the **Addressables** build process and create the required **AssetBundles**.

2. **Checking the created AssetBundles**
   After the build, check the folder specified in the **Build Path** for the corresponding group. It should contain the created **AssetBundles**.

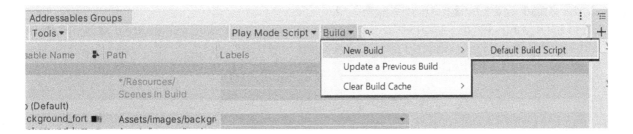

3. **Clearing Assemblies.**
   If this is not your first build, you should first clear the cache by clicking on the Build button and selecting *Clean Build Cache > All*. It is also recommended to clear previous builds in the folder, especially if you have had significant changes, it will help to protect you from unnecessary rubbish.

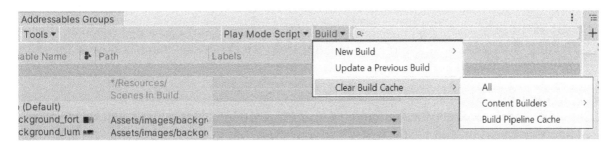

1.6 Addressables Local Hosting

If you plan to store AssetBundles not locally in a build, but on a CDN, which is the main goal of this task, but you don't have a CDN configured yet, local hosting comes to the rescue.
Local hosting allows you to use your computer as a server for Addressables, providing quick access to dynamically downloaded resources without having to deploy them to a remote server.
This is particularly useful during the development phase when you need to test Addressables on other devices (e.g. mobile devices), simulating the behaviour when downloading resources from the network.

Step 1: Enabling local hosting in Unity

To enable local hosting in Unity for Addressables:

1. **Open the Addressables Settings window:**
   In Unity, select *Window > Asset Management > Addressables > Groups.*

2. **Enable local hosting:**
   Click the **Hosting Services** tab in the **Addressables Groups** pane.
   Click **Create Hosting Service**, then select **Local Hosting**. This will create a local server for testing.

3. **Configure your hosting settings:**
   Under **Local Hosting Service**, you will see a URL that Unity automatically generates. This address will be used to access the resource from your device.

4. Check the Build and Load Path settings:
  Go to the settings for the **Addressables** group you want to test, and make sure that **Build Path** and **Load Path** are set correctly for local hosting.
  Make sure that **Load Path** points to the URL of the local server created in step 3.

Step 2: Build and test from a local server

To verify that Addressables works with the local server:

1. Create an Addressables build:
  Go to *Window > Asset Management > Addressables > Groups and select Build > New Build > Default Build Script*. This will create **AssetBundles** for the specified Addressables and prepare them for local hosting.

2. Start local hosting:
  In the **Hosting Services** panel, click Start **Hosting Service**. Your computer is now acting as a server and can be accessed at the specified URL.

3. Testing in the Unity editor:
  To ensure that addresses are loaded correctly, select **Play Mode Script** in the Addressables panel and set it to **Use Existing Build**. This will allow your project to load resources from local hosting instead of the Unity editor.

4. Work verification:
  Run the scene in **Play** mode in the Unity editor. If configured correctly, Addressables should load from the local server as if they were on the Internet.

Step 3: Testing on a mobile device via local hosting

Now, to test downloading Addressables from your mobile device, you need to follow a few extra steps so that your phone can access the local server on your computer:

- **Configure the local IP address:**
  - Determine the local IP address of your computer on the network. To do this, you can run the *ipconfig* (Windows) or *ifconfig* (macOS) command in the terminal. Find the line with your network name and IP address, for example *192.168.1.10.*
  - Go back to the Addressables settings and change **Load Path** to your IP address: for example, *http://192.168.1.10:port/*. The port can be found in the **Hosting Services** window.

- **Disabling the firewall (if required):**
  - To allow the device to connect to your computer, disable the firewall or add an exception for Unity.
  - On **Windows**: Go to *Control Panel > System and Security > Windows Firewall*, select **Allow an application or component through the Windows Firewall**, and add **Unity**.
  - On **macOS**: Go to *System Preferences > Security & Privacy > Firewall*, open **Firewall Settings**, and add **Unity**.

- **Run the test on a mobile device:**

  - Build the project for a mobile platform (iOS or Android) and install the application on your mobile device.
  - Make sure that both your computer and your phone are connected to the same Wi-Fi network. This is important because you can only access local hosting within the same network.
  - Launch the app on your phone. If everything is set up correctly, Addressables will be downloaded from your computer's local server.

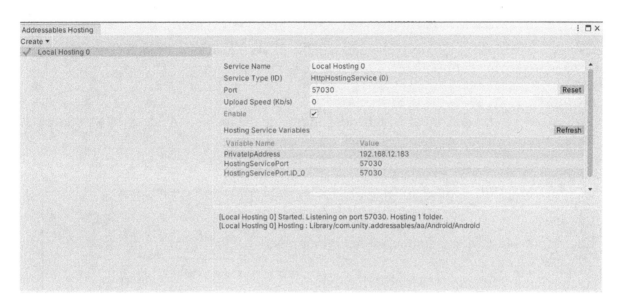

Tips and possible problems

- **Network problems:** If your phone can't see the server, try restarting Wi-Fi on both devices or checking your router settings.

- **Firewall problems:** If the problem persists after disabling the firewall, check your network settings - sometimes corporate or public networks restrict access between devices.

- **Hosting address:** If your computer's IP address has changed (for example, after a router reboot), be sure to update it in the **Load Path** settings in Unity.

  Local hosting is a powerful tool for fast debugging and testing Addressables on real devices. It allows you to save time on deployment and immediately see the result of the application as if the resources were downloaded from a real server.

Section 2: Basic scenarios for using Addressables

2.1. Loading and unloading of objects

Loading and unloading objects are fundamental operations when working with resources in Unity. Addressables greatly simplify these processes by providing convenient methods for managing the lifecycle of resources.

Object loading
With Addressables you can load objects by their address. This allows you to load resources only as needed, saving memory and improving performance.

Unloading of objects
Once an object is no longer needed, it can be unloaded to free up the memory it occupies. Addressables provide methods for efficient offloading of resources.

Example of loading and unloading an object:

```
using UnityEngine;
using UnityEngine.AddressableAssets;
using UnityEngine.ResourceManagement.AsyncOperations;

public class UnloadObjectExample : MonoBehaviour
{
    // Addressable resource address
    public string objectAddress;
    private AsyncOperationHandle<GameObject> handle;

    void Start()
    {
        // Asynchronous object loading
        handle = Addressables.LoadAssetAsync<GameObject>(objectAddress);
        handle.Completed += OnLoadDone;
    }

    void OnLoadDone(AsyncOperationHandle<GameObject> loadedHandle)
    {
        if (loadedHandle.Status == AsyncOperationStatus.Succeeded)
        {
            // Instantiating a loaded object in a scene
            GameObject obj = Instantiate(loadedHandle.Result);
            //We launch a coroutine to demonstrate unloading after 5 seconds
            StartCoroutine(UnloadAfterDelay(obj, 5f));
        }
        else
        {
            Debug.LogError("Failed to load object at address: " + objectAddress);
```

```
      }
   }

   System.Collections.IEnumerator UnloadAfterDelay(GameObject obj, float delay)
   {

      yield return new WaitForSeconds(delay);
      // Removing an object from the scene
      Destroy(obj);
      //Unloading an Addressable resource
      Addressables.Release(handle);
      Debug.Log("Unloading an Addressable resource.");
   }
}
```

Code Explanation:
- **objectAddress** - a string containing the Addressable address of the resource to be loaded.
- **LoadAssetAsync<GameObject>** — method for asynchronous loading of a game object.
- **OnLoadDone** — handler method that is called after the download is complete. If the load is successful, the object is instantiated in the scene.
- **handle** — stores a link to the downloaded resource.

After the object is instantiated, a coroutine is run that removes the object from the scene after a given delay and calls Addressables.Release to unload the resource.

2.2. Addressable Asset Labels: multi-resource management

Labels (The Addressables system allows you to group related resources under a common identifier. This makes it easier to manage and load multiple resources at the same time.

Assigning labels to resources

Tags can be assigned to resources either through the Unity Editor interface or programmatically.

Tag assignment via Unity Editor:
1. Open the window **Addressables Groups**: *Window > Asset Management > Addressables > Groups.*
2. Select a resource or group of resources.
3. In the inspector, find the field **Labels** and add a new label or select an existing label.

Example of assigning a label programmatically:

```
using UnityEngine;
using UnityEngine.AddressableAssets;
using UnityEngine.ResourceManagement.AsyncOperations;

public class AssignLabelExample : MonoBehaviour
```

```
{
    public AssetReference assetReference;
    public string newLabel = "Environment"

    void Start()
    {

        // Adding a tag to a resource
        Addressables.AddLabel(newLabel, assetReference.RuntimeKey.ToString());
        Debug.Log(The object is unloaded and memory is freed);
    }
}
```

Explanation of the code:
- **AssetReference** — Addressable resource link.
- **AddLabel** — method for adding a label to a resource by its key.

Loading resources by tag

Using labels allows you to load groups of resources simultaneously, which is especially useful when working with multiple related objects.

Example of downloading all resources with a specific label:

```
using UnityEngine;
using UnityEngine.AddressableAssets;
using UnityEngine.ResourceManagement.AsyncOperations;
using System.Collections.Generic;

public class LoadByLabelExample : MonoBehaviour
{
    public string labelToLoad = "Environment";

    void Start()
    {
        // Adding a tag to a resource
        Addressables.LoadAssetsAsync<GameObject>(labelToLoad, OnAssetLoaded)
        .Completed += OnLoadDone;
    }
    void OnAssetLoaded(GameObject obj)
    {
        // Instantiating a Loaded Object
        Instantiate(obj);
    }

    void OnLoadDone(AsyncOperationHandle<IList<GameObject>> handle)
    {
        if (handle.Status == AsyncOperationStatus.Succeeded)
```

```
    {
        Debug.Log("All resources with label '" + labelToLoad + "' have been successfully
loaded and instantiated.");
    }
    else
    {
        Debug.LogError("Failed to load resources with label:" + labelToLoad);
    }
}
void OnDestroy()
{
    // Unloading all loaded resources when an object is destroyed
    Addressables.Release(handle);
}
}
```

Explanation of the code:
- **LoadAssetsAsync<GameObject>** — method to load all resources of **GameObject** type having the specified label.
- **OnAssetLoaded** — is called for each loaded object where it is instantiated in the scene.
- **OnLoadDone** — is called after all resources have been loaded, checks the operation status.

2.3. Asynchronous loading withAddressables

Asynchronous resource loading allows content to be loaded in the background without blocking the main flow of the game. This is especially important to ensure smooth operation of the application and prevent delays when loading large resources.

2.3.1. Advantages of asynchronous loading.

- **Smooth application performance:** avoiding freezes and delays during resource loading.

- **Performance optimisation:** the ability to load resources as needed, spreading the load on CPU and memory.

- **Improved user experience:** responsive interface and no lag when switching scenes or loading content.

2.3.2. Using coroutines for asynchronous loading

Coroutines in Unity allow asynchronous operations to be performed sequentially, making it easier to manage resource utilisation. You can implement the task via coroutines as follows:

```
IEnumerator LoadObjectCoroutine(string address)
{
    AsyncOperationHandle<GameObject> handle = Addressables
    .LoadAssetAsync<GameObject>(address);
```

```
    // Waiting for download to complete
    yield return handle;
    if (handle.Status == AsyncOperationStatus.Succeeded)
    {

        // Instantiating a Loaded Object
        Instantiate(handle.Result);
        Debug.Log("Object loaded successfully via coroutine.");
    }
    else
    {
        Debug.LogError("Failed to load object at address: " + address);
    }
  }
  void OnDestroy()
  {

      // Unloading a resource when an object is destroyed
      Addressables.Release(handle);
  }
}
```

Explanation of the code:
- The **LoadObjectCoroutine** starts loading a resource and waits for it to complete with the *yield return handle.*
- Once the upload is complete, the status of the operation is checked, and if successful, the object is instantiated.
- In the **OnDestroy** method, **Addressables.Release** is called to release the resource.

It is important to properly handle possible resource loading errors to prevent application crashes and provide informative messages to the user.

2.3.3. Using Task for asynchronous loading

Instead of coroutine, you can use, **Task** from namespace **System.Threading.Tasks** provides a more modern and flexible approach to managing asynchronous operations. Utilisation **Task** allows you to take advantage of async/await syntax, making code more readable and maintainable.

Advantages of use **Task**:

- **Readability:** async/await makes asynchronous code look like synchronous code, making it easier to understand the logic.
- **Error handling:** Exceptions can be handled using standard try-catch mechanisms.
- **Task Composition:** Easy merging of multiple asynchronous operations.

Example of using **Task** to load an **Addressable** resource:

```
using System.Threading.Tasks;
using UnityEngine;
using UnityEngine.AddressableAssets;
using UnityEngine.ResourceManagement.AsyncOperations;
```

```csharp
public class TaskLoadExample : MonoBehaviour
{
  //Addressable resource address
   public string objectAddress;
   async void Start()
   {
     try
     {
       // Loading a resource asynchronously using Task
       GameObject loadedObject = await LoadAssetAsync<GameObject>(objectAddress);
       Instantiate(loadedObject);
       Debug.Log("The object was successfully loaded and instantiated using Task.");
     }
     catch (System.Exception ex)
     {
       Debug.LogError($"Error loading object at address {objectAddress}: {ex.Message}");
     }
   }
   //Method to load an Addressable resource using Task
   public Task<T> LoadAssetAsync<T>(string address) where T : class
   {
     var tcs = new TaskCompletionSource<T>();
     AsyncOperationHandle<T> handle = Addressables.LoadAssetAsync<T>(address);
     handle.Completed += (operation) =>
     {
       if (operation.Status == AsyncOperationStatus.Succeeded)
       {
         tcs.SetResult(operation.Result);
       }
       else
       {
         tcs.SetException(new System.Exception("Could not load resource."));
       }
     };
     return tcs.Task;
   }

   void OnDestroy()
   {
     // Optional: Unloading a resource when an object is destroyed
     Addressables.ReleaseInstance(gameObject);
   }
}
```

Code Explanation:

- **LoadAssetAsync<T>**: A generic method that returns **Task<T>**, allowing you to use await to load resources.
- **try-catch**: Handling possible exceptions when loading a resource.
- **Instantiate**: Creating an instance of the loaded object in the scene.

Important points:

- **TaskCompletionSource**: It's used to convert **AsyncOperationHandle** in Task, which allows Addressables to be integrated with async/await.

- **Lifecycle management:** Don't forget to offload resources using Addressables.Release or Addressables.ReleaseInstance to avoid memory leaks.

2.3.4. Using UniTask for asynchronous loading

UniTask — is a third-party library developed by Cysharp that provides high-performance asynchronous operations for Unity. It is particularly useful for projects where maximum performance and minimal rubbish collector overhead are required. It is also a great advantage over Task for use on the platform Web.

Advantages of use **UniTask**:

- **Performance:** Less memory allocation and better performance compared to traditional **Task**.
- **Unity integration:** Specially designed for Unity, supports coroutines and other engine features.
- **Async/await support: Allows you to write clean and clear asynchronous code.**

InstallationUniTask:

1. **Through Unity-Paketmanager:**
   Open Package **Manager** (*Window > Package Manager*).
   Press the + sign and select**Add package from git URL....**
   Enter URL: **https://github.com/Cysharp/UniTask.git#upm**
   Click **Add**.

2. **Via Git:**
   Add **https://github.com/Cysharp/UniTask.git#upm** depending on your project.

Example of using **UniTask** to load an **Addressable** resource:

```
using UnityEngine;
using UnityEngine.AddressableAssets;
using UnityEngine.ResourceManagement.AsyncOperations;
using Cysharp.Threading.Tasks;

public class UniTaskLoadExample : MonoBehaviour
{
    // The address of an Addressable resource
    public string objectAddress;

    async void Start()
```

```csharp
{
    try
    {
        // Loading a resource asynchronously using UniTask
        GameObject loadedObject = await LoadAssetAsync<GameObject>(objectAddress);
        Instantiate(loadedObject);
        Debug.Log("The object was successfully loaded and instantiated using UniTask.");
    }
    catch (System.Exception ex)
    {
        Debug.LogError($"Error loading object at address {objectAddress}: {ex.Message}");
    }
}

// Method to load an Addressable resource using UniTask
public async UniTask<T> LoadAssetAsync<T>(string address) where T : class
{
    AsyncOperationHandle<T> handle = Addressables.LoadAssetAsync<T>(address);
    await handle.Task;

    if (handle.Status == AsyncOperationStatus.Succeeded)
    {
        return handle.Result;
    }
    else
    {
        throw new System.Exception("Failed to load resource.");
    }
}

void OnDestroy()
{
    // Optional: Unloading a resource when an object is destroyed
    Addressables.ReleaseInstance(gameObject);
}
}
```

Explanation of the code:
- **LoadAssetAsync<T>**: The method uses **UniTask** to load the resource asynchronously.
- **await handle.Task**: Asynchronous waiting for download completion.
- **throw**: Generating an exception on failed load that can be handled in try-catch.

Important points:

- **Minimise rubbish collection: UniTask** is optimised to reduce memory allocation, which is especially important for mobile and high-performance applications.

- **Integration with Unity API: UniTask** provides extensions and utilities to work with various aspects of Unity, such as coroutines and events.

Additional **UniTask** features:

- **Cancellation of tasks:** Support for cancellation tokens to interrupt asynchronous operations.
- **Combining tasks:** Ability to combine multiple UniTasks for parallel or sequential execution.

```csharp
using UnityEngine;
using Cysharp.Threading.Tasks;

public class UniTaskMultipleLoadExample : MonoBehaviour
{
    public string firstAssetAddress;
    public string secondAssetAddress;

    async void Start()
    {
        try
        {
            // Loading two resources in parallel
            var loadFirst = LoadAssetAsync<GameObject>(firstAssetAddress);
            var loadSecond = LoadAssetAsync<GameObject>(secondAssetAddress);
            await UniTask.WhenAll(loadFirst, loadSecond);
            Instantiate(loadFirst.Result);
            Instantiate(loadSecond.Result);
            Debug.Log("Both objects were successfully loaded and instantiated using UniTask.");
        }
        catch (System.Exception ex)
        {
            Debug.LogError($Error loading resources: {ex.Message}");
        }
    }

    public async UniTask<T> LoadAssetAsync<T>(string address) where T : class
    {
        var handle = Addressables.LoadAssetAsync<T>(address);
        await handle.Task;
        if (handle.Status == AsyncOperationStatus.Succeeded)
        {
            return handle.Result;
        }
        else
        {
            throw new System.Exception($"Failed to load resource at address {address}.");
        }
```

```
    }

    void OnDestroy()
    {
        // Optional: Unloading a resource when an object is destroyed
        Addressables.ReleaseInstance(gameObject);
    }
}
```

Explanation of the code:
- **UniTask.WhenAll**: The method allows you to wait for the completion of all transferred tasks.
- **Parallel Loading:** Loading multiple resources at the same time, which can reduce the overall loading time.

2.3.5 Recommendations when using Task and UniTask:

1. **Choice of approach**:
   - Use **Task** for simple asynchronous operations and when you need compatibility with existing C# code. At the time of writing, the Web platform does not support **Task**.
   - Use **UniTask** in projects where high performance and minimising rubbish collection are important. Also, if you are considering the Web platform.

2. **Error handling**:
   - Always handle possible exceptions when loading resources to prevent application crashes.

3. **Resource lifecycle management**:
   - Don't forget to unload resources after using them with the Addressables.Release or Addressables.ReleaseInstance.

4. **Combining with other systems**:
   - **UniTask** integrates well with other libraries and systems such as DI containers or state management systems.

2.4. Resource dependency management

Addressables automatically manage dependencies between resources, making them easy to load and unload. However, understanding this mechanism is important for optimal handling of resources.

2.4.1. Automatic dependency management

When Addressables loads a resource, it also automatically loads all of its dependencies. This ensures that all required components of the resource are available.

Example of unloading:

```
System.Collections.IEnumerator UnloadAfterDelay(GameObject character, float delay)
{
    yield return new WaitForSeconds(delay);
    Destroy(character);
    Addressables.Release(handle);
    Debug.Log("The character and its dependencies are unloaded from memory.");
}
```

Explanation of the code:

- To remove a character from the scene, **Addressables.Release** is called, which unloads both the character itself and its dependencies (materials, textures, etc.) if they are no longer used anywhere else.

Suppose you have a character prefab that depends on several materials and textures. When you load this prefab via Addressables, all related materials and textures will be loaded automatically.

But if you have another enemy prefab, such as a "skeleton" - and it uses some of the same sprites or materials, but is in a different bundle.

Let's look at two problems:

- The first is each bundle contains a duplicate - and increases the uploads.
- Second, when destroying an enemy - we want to unload it from memory - and it has connections, and as long as the connections are used - it is not unloaded..

This is only a visible part of the possible problems. Which can be easily fixed by removing dependencies between bundles or combining them into a single bundle depending on your situation.

2.5. Loading scenes using Addressables

Addressables allow you to load and unload scenes asynchronously, which is especially useful for managing large projects with multiple levels or locations.

2.5.1. Adding scenes to Addressables

Before you can load a scene via Addressables, you must add it to the systemAddressables:

1. Open the window **Addressables Groups**: *Window > Asset Management > Addressables > Groups.*

2. Drag the scene from **Project Window** in the right group **Addressables**.

3. Make sure that the scene is assigned a unique address (address).

2.5.2. Asynchronous scene loading

Example of loading a scene asynchronously:

```
public string currentSceneAddress;
 public string nextSceneAddress;
   System.Collections.IEnumerator LoadSceneAsync(string address)
   {
     AsyncOperationHandle<SceneInstance> handle =
Addressables.LoadSceneAsync(address, LoadSceneMode.Additive);
     yield return handle;
     if (handle.Status == AsyncOperationStatus.Succeeded)
     {
        Debug.Log("Scene '" + address + "' successfully loaded");
     }
     else
     {
        Debug.LogError("Failed to load scene at: " + address);
     }
   }
   void OnDestroy()
   {
     Addressables.UnloadSceneAsync(handle, true);
   }
```

Explanation of the code:
- **LoadSceneAsync** loads a scene asynchronously in Additive mode, which allows you to add it to already loaded scenes.
- When a scene is unloaded, UnloadSceneAsync is called, which can also unload related resources.

2.5.3. Controlling transitions between scenes

Using Addressables to load scenes allows for more flexibility in managing transitions between levels, allowing for smooth, lag-free loading and unloading.

Example of a smooth transition between scenes:

```
   System.Collections.IEnumerator TransitionToNextScene()
   {
     //Asynchronously unloading the current scene
     AsyncOperationHandle<SceneInstance> unloadHandle =
Addressables.UnloadSceneAsync(currentSceneAddress);
     yield return unloadHandle;

     if (unloadHandle.Status == AsyncOperationStatus.Succeeded)
     {
        Debug.Log("The current scene has been successfully unloaded.");
```

```
    // Loading the next scene asynchronously
    AsyncOperationHandle<SceneInstance> loadHandle =
Addressables.LoadSceneAsync(nextSceneAddress, LoadSceneMode.Single);
    yield return loadHandle;

    if (loadHandle.Status == AsyncOperationStatus.Succeeded)
    {
       Debug.Log("The next scene has loaded successfully.");
    }
    else
    {
       Debug.LogError("Failed to load the following scene at: " + nextSceneAddress);
    }
  }
  else
  {
     Debug.LogError("Failed to unload the current scene at: " + currentSceneAddress);
  }
}
```

Explanation of the code:
- First the current scene is unloaded, then a new scene is loaded in Single mode, replacing the previous scene.
- This approach ensures smooth transitions between levels without lags and freezes.

2.6. Using Addressables to dynamically update content

Addressables allow you to update game content without having to release a full app update. This is especially useful for mobile games and apps where it is important to respond quickly to changes and add new content.

2.6.1. Hosting resources on a remote server

To dynamically update content, you must host AssetBundles on a remote server. Then configure Addressables to load resources from this server.

Steps to configure remote storage:

1. **Placing AssetBundles on the server:**
   - After building Addressables, select the assembled AssetBundles and upload them to your server or CDN.

2. **Configuring the Addressables profile for the remote path:**

  - In the Addressables Groups window, go to Profile and set the RemoteBuildPath and RemoteLoadPath variables to the URL of your server.

3. **Changing group settings to use remote paths:**

  - Select the Addressables group you want to store remotely.

  - In the inspector, configure Build Path and Load Path using profile variables such as ${RemoteBuildPath} and ${RemoteLoadPath}.

2.6.2. Dynamic loading of updated content

Once remote storage is set up, you can download updated resources as needed.

```
public string remoteAssetAddress;
void Start()
{
    // Asynchronous loading of an updated resource from a remote server
    Addressables.LoadAssetAsync<GameObject>(remoteAssetAddress)
    .Completed += OnAssetLoaded;
}
void OnAssetLoaded(AsyncOperationHandle<GameObject> handle)
{
    if (handle.Status == AsyncOperationStatus.Succeeded)
    {
        Instantiate(handle.Result);
        Debug.Log("The updated resource has been successfully loaded and instantiated..");
    }
    else
    {
        Debug.LogError("Failed to load updated asset at: " + remoteAssetAddress);
    }
}
void OnDestroy()
{
    Addressables.Release(handle);
}
```

2.6.3. Updating content after the release of an application

Addressables make it easy to deploy content updates after an app is released. All you need to do is update the resources on the server and ensure that the application downloads them from a remote path.

Steps to update your content:
1. Build and upload updated AssetBundles to the server.
2. Updating the Addressables profile when necessary.

3. Restarting the application or running the update mechanism within the application to load new resources.

Example of a mechanism for checking and downloading updates:

```csharp
void Start()=>   CheckForUpdates();

void CheckForUpdates()
{
    Addressables.CheckForCatalogUpdates().Completed += OnCheckForUpdates;
}

void OnCheckForUpdates(AsyncOperationHandle<System.Collections.Generic
    .IList<string>> handle)
{
    if (handle.Status == AsyncOperationStatus.Succeeded && handle.Result.Count > 0)
    {
        Debug.Log("Catalog updates found. The download of updates begins.");
        Addressables.UpdateCatalogs(handle.Result).Completed += OnUpdateCatalogs;
    }
    else
    {
        Debug.Log("No catalog updates found.");
    }
}

void OnUpdateCatalogs(AsyncOperationHandle<System.Collections
    .Generic.IList<string>> handle)
{
    if (handle.Status == AsyncOperationStatus.Succeeded)
    {
        Debug.Log("The catalogs have been successfully updated.");
        // After updating the directories, you can download new resources
    }
    else
    {
        Debug.LogError("Failed to update directories");
    }
}
```

Explanation of the code:
- **CheckForCatalogUpdates** checks for Addressables directory updates on the server.
- If updates are found, UpdateCatalogs downloads them, after which new or updated resources can be downloaded.

2.7. Resource versioning management

Proper version management of resources is important to ensure compatibility and prevent conflicts when updating content.

2.7.1. The use of versions inAddressables

Addressables support resource versioning, which allows you to track changes and manage updates. Steps for version control:

1. Setting the version in the profile**Addressables**:
   - In the Addressables Groups window, open**Profiles**.
   - Add or modify versioning-related variables such as BuildPath and LoadPath to include the version number.

2. Build and publish new versions **AssetBundles**:
   - Increase the version number each time resources are updated.
   - Collect and upload new **AssetBundles** to the server with a new version-appropriate path.

3. Version-aware resource loading:
   - The application must know the current version and load resources from the appropriate path.

Example of using profile variables for a version:

```
// Variables are created in the profile, for example:
// BuildPath = "AssetBundles/v1"
// LoadPath = "https://yourserver.com/AssetBundles/v1"


  public string version = "v1";
  public string assetAddress;

void Start()
  {
    // Setting the current profile version
    Addressables.RuntimePath = "https://yourserver.com/AssetBundles/" + version;
    // Asynchronous resource loading
    Addressables.LoadAssetAsync<GameObject>(assetAddress).Completed +=
OnAssetLoaded;
  }

  void OnAssetLoaded(UnityEngine.ResourceManagement
      .AsyncOperations.AsyncOperationHandle<GameObject> handle)
  {
    if (handle.Status == UnityEngine.ResourceManagement
      .AsyncOperations.AsyncOperationStatus.Succeeded)
    {
      Instantiate(handle.Result);
```

```
        Debug.Log("Resource loaded from version: " + version);
      }
      else
      {
        Debug.LogError("Failed to load resource from version: " + version);
      }
    }

  void OnDestroy()
  {
    Addressables.Release(handle);
  }
}
```

Explanation of the code:
- RuntimePath is set to the path corresponding to the current version.
- When the version changes, the application must update the RuntimePath to load resources from the new path.

2.7.2. Version compatibility management

When updating resources, it is important to ensure compatibility between different versions, especially if the application is already installed by users.

Recommendations:
- Save older versions on the server for a certain period of time so that users can continue to use older versions of the application without conflicts.
- Use migrations to update data or resources if the structure has changed.
- Test updates on different versions of the app to make sure it works correctly.

2.8. Monitoring and analytics of utilisation Addressables

For optimal performance with Addressables, it is useful to monitor resource usage, data loads, and performance.

2.8.1. Integration with analytics systems

Addressables' integration with analytics systems allows you to collect data on resource utilisation, load times and other metrics.

Example of sending data on resource load to the analytics system:

```
void OnAssetLoaded(AsyncOperationHandle<GameObject> handle)
  {
    if (handle.Status == AsyncOperationStatus.Succeeded)
```

```
        {
            Instantiate(handle.Result);
            Debug.Log("Resource loaded successfully.");
            // Sending an event to the analytics system
            SendAnalyticsEvent("AssetLoaded", assetAddress);
        }
        else
        {
            Debug.LogError("Failed to load resource..");
            // Sending an error event
            SendAnalyticsEvent("AssetLoadFailed", assetAddress);
        }
    }

    void SendAnalyticsEvent(string eventName, string asset)
    {
        // Example of sending an event (replace with your analytics system
        Debug.Log($"Analytics Event: {eventName} | Asset: {asset}");
        // For example, for use with Unity Analytics:
        // Analytics.CustomEvent(eventName, new Dictionary<string, object> { { "Asset", asset
} });
    }
```

Explanation of the code:
- When a resource is loaded, an event is sent to the analytics system with information about the load.
- This allows you to track which resources are being downloaded most frequently, as well as identify download problems.

2.8.2. Optimisation based on analytical data

The data collected can be used to optimise the use of Addressables:
- Analyse frequently used resources and group them to speed up utilisation.
- Identify infrequently used resources and consider removing or optimising them.
- Monitor load times and look for ways to reduce them, for example by reducing the size of AssetBundles or optimising their structure.

2.9 Loading progress

During loading sometimes it is necessary to display the loading progress, say for the progress bar during the start of the game or somewhere in the transitions.

38

Download example:

```
using Cysharp.Threading.Tasks;
using UnityEngine;
using UnityEngine.AddressableAssets;

public class LoadingProgressTracker
{
    public float Progress { get; private set; }

    public async UniTask TrackProgress(string label)
    {
        Debug.Log($"[LoadingProgressTracker] I'm starting to track the download progress for
the label: {label}");
        var handle = Addressables.LoadAssetsAsync<object>(label, null);

        while (!handle.IsDone)
        {
            Progress = handle.PercentComplete;
            Debug.Log($"[LoadingProgressTracker] Progress: {Progress * 100}%");
            await UniTask.Yield();
        }

        Debug.Log("[LoadingProgressTracker] Download complete.");
        Addressables.Release(handle);
    }
}
```

If you want to show progress in more detail, you can use the following code.

```
using System.Collections.Generic;
using UnityEngine;
using UnityEngine.AddressableAssets;
using UnityEngine.ResourceManagement.AsyncOperations;

public class LoadingProgressTracker
{
    public float Progress { get; private set; }
    public long DownloadedBytes { get; private set; }
    public long TotalBytes { get; private set; }
    public string CurrentFile { get; private set; }

    private List<AsyncOperationHandle> _currentHandles = new();

    public async UniTask TrackProgressWithDetails(string label)
```

```csharp
    {
        Debug.Log($"[LoadingProgressTracker]Starting to track upload progress for the label:
{label}");

        // Preparing the download
        AsyncOperationHandle<long> sizeHandle = Addressables
        .GetDownloadSizeAsync(label);

        await sizeHandle.ToUniTask();

        if (sizeHandle.Status == AsyncOperationStatus.Failed || sizeHandle.Result <= 0)
        {
            Debug.Log($"[Loading Progress Tracker] There is no download required for the
label '{label}'.");
            return;
        }

        TotalBytes = sizeHandle.Result;
        Debug.Log($"[LoadingProgressTracker] Total to download: {TotalBytes / (1024 *
1024f):F2} MB");

        // Start downloading
        var handle = Addressables.DownloadDependenciesAsync(label, true);
        _currentHandles.Add(handle);

        while (!handle.IsDone)
        {
            Progress = handle.PercentComplete;
            DownloadedBytes = (long)(TotalBytes * Progress);
            CurrentFile = GetCurrentFileFromHandle(handle);

            Debug.Log($"[LoadingProgressTracker] Progress: {Progress * 100:F1}%, " +
                    $"Downloaded: {DownloadedBytes / (1024 * 1024f):F2} MB / {TotalBytes /
(1024 * 1024f):F2} MB, " +  $"File.: {CurrentFile}");

            await UniTask.Yield();
        }
        // Finish loading
        Debug.Log($"[Loading Progress Tracker] Loading completed for label '{label}'.");
        Addressables.Release(sizeHandle);
        Addressables.Release(handle);
    }

    private string GetCurrentFileFromHandle(AsyncOperationHandle handle)
    {
        if (handle.DebugName != null)
```

```
    {
        return handle.DebugName;
    }
    return "Unknown file";
  }
}
```

What's new:

1. Getting the total size: Use Addressables.GetDownloadSizeAsync to get the total amount of downloaded data.

2. Dynamic update of current file: Added GetCurrentFileFromHandle method to retrieve information about the currently loaded file.

3. Display progress in MB: The log includes downloaded data and total size in megabytes.

Console output example:

```
[LoadingProgressTracker] Total download: 10.25 MB
[LoadingProgressTracker] Progress: 25.3%, Downloaded: 2.59 MB / 10.25 MB, File: Atlas.asset
[LoadingProgressTracker] Progress: 50.1%, Downloaded: 5.13 MB / 10.25 MB, File: Music.asset
[LoadingProgressTracker] Progress: 100.0%, Downloaded: 10.25 MB / 10.25 MB, File: Prefab.asset
[LoadingProgressTracker] Loading completed for 'EventLabel'.
```

Conclusion of the section

In this section, we covered the main scenarios for using Addressables in Unity, including loading and unloading objects, labelled resource management, asynchronous loading, dependency management, loading scenes, dynamically updating content, and monitoring resource usage. Understanding and correctly applying these scenarios will allow you to effectively use Addressables to optimise your project, improve performance and provide flexibility in resource management.

Section 3: Examples of loading different types of data

In this section, we'll look at a few practical examples of how to use Addressables in Unity. These examples will help you understand how to effectively integrate Addressables into your project and use them to manage different types of resources.

3.1. Loading sprites using Addressables

Sprites are often used in 2D games to represent characters, objects, and interface elements. Addressables allow you to dynamically load sprites as needed, optimising memory usage and improving performance.

Steps to load a sprite:

1. **Sprite call inAddressables:**
   - Drag the desired sprite from the **Project Window** to the desired group in the window **Addressables Groups**.
   - Make sure the sprite has a unique address. You can change the address in the inspector to make it more descriptive and structured.

2. **Creating a script to load a sprite:**

Create a new C# script, such as **SpriteLoader.cs**, and add it to the desired object in the scene.

```csharp
using UnityEngine;
using UnityEngine.AddressableAssets;
using UnityEngine.ResourceManagement.AsyncOperations;

public class SpriteLoader : MonoBehaviour
{
    public string spriteAddress; // Unique sprite address in Addressables
    public SpriteRenderer spriteRenderer; // SpriteRenderer component for displaying a sprite
    private AsyncOperationHandle<Sprite> handle;

    void Start()
    {
        // SpriteRenderer component for displaying a sprite
        handle = Addressables.LoadAssetAsync<Sprite>(spriteAddress);
        handle.Completed += OnSpriteLoaded;
    }

    void OnSpriteLoaded(AsyncOperationHandle<Sprite> handle)
    {
        if (handle.Status == AsyncOperationStatus.Succeeded)
```

```
    {
      // Setting the downloaded sprite to SpriteRenderer
      spriteRenderer.sprite = handle.Result;
      Debug.Log("The sprite has been successfully downloaded and installed.");
    }
    else
    {
      Debug.LogError($"Failed to load sprite at:{spriteAddress}");
    }
  }

  void OnDestroy()
  {
    //Unloading a sprite when an object is destroyed
    Addressables.Release(handle);
  }
}
```

Explanation of the code:
- **spriteAddress** — a string containing the Addressable address of the sprite to be loaded.
- **spriteRenderer** — reference to the SpriteRenderer component where the loaded sprite will be installed.
- **LoadAssetAsync<Sprite>** — method for asynchronous sprite loading.
- **OnSpriteLoaded** — handler method that is called after the download is complete. If the download is successful, the sprite is set to **SpriteRenderer**.

3. **Scene Setup:**
   - Add a **SpriteLoader** component to an object in the scene.
   - In the inspector, specify **spriteAddress** — sprite address in **Addressables**.
   - Assign a link to **SpriteRenderer**, where the sprite will be placed.

4. **Load testing:**
   - Run the scene and make sure the sprite loads and displays correctly.
   - Check the console for successful boot or error messages.

3.2. Loading 3D models using Addressables

Loading 3D models is similar to loading sprites, but requires some additional settings.

Steps to load a 3D model:

1. **Adding a 3D model toAddressables:**
   - Drag the 3D model from the **Project Window** to the desired group in the window **Addressables Groups**.
   - Make sure the model has a unique address.

2. Creating a script to load a 3D model:

Create a new C# script, such as **ModelLoader.cs**, and add it to the desired object in the scene.

```csharp
using UnityEngine;
using UnityEngine.AddressableAssets;
using UnityEngine.ResourceManagement.AsyncOperations;
using Cysharp.Threading.Tasks; //If you use UniTask

public class ModelLoader : MonoBehaviour
{
// Unique address of the model in Addressables
    public string modelAddress;

    async void Start()
    {
      try
      {
        // Asynchronous model loading
        GameObject model = await Addressables
            .LoadAssetAsync<GameObject>(modelAddress).Task;

        Instantiate(model, transform.position, transform.rotation);
        Debug.Log("The 3D model has been successfully loaded and instantiated.");
      }
      catch (System.Exception ex)
      {
        Debug.LogError($"Error loading model at address {modelAddress}:
{ex.Message}");
      }
    }
  void OnDestroy()
  {
    // Optional: Unloading the model when an object is destroyed
    Addressables.ReleaseInstance(gameObject);
  }
}
```

Explanation of the code:
- Using async/await makes asynchronous model loading easier.
- **LoadAssetAsync<GameObject>** — method for loading a 3D model.
- The model is instantiated in the position and rotation of the object to which the script is attached.

3. Scene Setup:
- Add a **ModelLoader** component to an object in the scene.

- In the inspector, specify **modelAddress** - the address of the model in Addressables.

4. **Load testing:**
    - Run the scene and make sure the model loads and displays correctly.
    - Check the console for successful boot or error messages.

3.3. Uploading audio using Addressables

Addressables allow you to control the loading and playback of audio resources, which is useful for dynamically controlling the sound in a game.

Steps for downloading audio:

1. **Adding an audio file to Addressables:**
    - Drag the audio file from **Project Window** to the desired group in the window **Addressables Groups**.
    - Make sure the audio file has a unique address.

2. **Creating a script to download and play audio:**

Create a new C# script, such as **AudioLoader.cs**, and add it to the desired object in the scene.

```
using UnityEngine;
using UnityEngine.AddressableAssets;
using UnityEngine.ResourceManagement.AsyncOperations;

public class AudioLoader : MonoBehaviour
{
  // Unique address of the audio file in Addressables
  public string audioAddress;
  private AudioSource audioSource;
  private AsyncOperationHandle<AudioClip> handle;

  void Start()
  {
    audioSource = gameObject.AddComponent<AudioSource>();
  // Asynchronous audio loading
    handle = Addressables.LoadAssetAsync<AudioClip>(audioAddress);
    handle.Completed += OnAudioLoaded;
  }

  void OnAudioLoaded(AsyncOperationHandle<AudioClip> handle)
  {
    if (handle.Status == AsyncOperationStatus.Succeeded)
    {
      // Set the downloaded audio to AudioSource and play it
```

```
      audioSource.clip = handle.Result;
      audioSource.Play();
      Debug.Log("The audio has been successfully downloaded and is playing.");
    }
    else
    {
      Debug.LogError($"Failed to load audio at:{audioAddress}");
    }
  }

  void OnDestroy()
  {
    // Upload audio when object is destroyed
    Addressables.Release(handle);
  }
}
```

Explanation of the code:
- **audioAddress** — a string containing the address of the Addressable audio file.
- **AudioSource** — audio playback component.
- **LoadAssetAsync<AudioClip>** — method for downloading an audio file.
- **OnAudioLoaded** — handler method that sets the downloaded audio to AudioSource and plays it back.

3. **Scene Setup:**
   - Add an AudioLoader component to an object in the scene.
   - In the inspector, specify audioAddress - the address of the audio file in Addressables.

4. **Load testing:**
   - Release the scene and make sure that the audio file is loaded and played back.
   - Check the console for successful boot or error messages.

If it's **Unitask**, here's an option:

```
using UnityEngine;
using UnityEngine.AddressableAssets;
using UnityEngine.ResourceManagement.AsyncOperations;
using Cysharp.Threading.Tasks;

public class UniTaskAudioManager : MonoBehaviour
{
  public string audioAddress;
  private AudioSource audioSource;
  private AsyncOperationHandle<AudioClip> audioHandle;

  void Start()
  {
```

```
      audioSource = gameObject.AddComponent<AudioSource>();
      LoadAndPlayAudio().Forget();
   }

   private async UniTaskVoid LoadAndPlayAudio()
   {
      try
      {
         audioHandle = Addressables.LoadAssetAsync<AudioClip>(audioAddress);
         await audioHandle.Task;
         if (audioHandle.Status == AsyncOperationStatus.Succeeded)
         {
            audioSource.clip = audioHandle.Result;
            audioSource.Play();
            Debug.Log("The audio has been successfully downloaded and is playing.");
         }
         else
         {
            Debug.LogError($""Failed to load audio at: {audioAddress}");
         }
      }
      catch (System.Exception ex)
      {
         Debug.LogError($"Error loading audio:{ex.Message}");
      }
   }

   void OnDestroy()
   {
      Addressables.Release(audioHandle);
   }
}
```

Explanation of the code:
- Using UniTaskVoid for an asynchronous method that does not return a value.
- The LoadAndPlayAudio method loads an audio resource and plays it back.
- The audio resource is unloaded when the object is destroyed.

3.4. Loading scenes using Addressables

Addressables allow you to control the loading and unloading of scenes asynchronously, which is useful for creating multi-level games and managing resources during transitions between scenes.

Steps to load a scene:

1. Adding a scene to Addressables:
   - Drag the scene from the **Project Window** to the desired group in the **Addressables Groups** window.
   - Make sure the scene has a unique address.

2. Creating a script to load a scene:

Create a new C# script, such as **SceneLoader.cs**, and add it to the object in the scene.

```csharp
using UnityEngine;
using UnityEngine.AddressableAssets;
using UnityEngine.ResourceManagement.AsyncOperations;
using UnityEngine.SceneManagement;
using Cysharp.Threading.Tasks;  //If you use UniTask


public class SceneLoader : MonoBehaviour
{
 // Unique scene address in Addressables
   public string sceneAddress;

   async void Start()
   {
     try
     {
       //Asynchronous scene loading
       SceneInstance scene = await Addressables
         .LoadSceneAsync(sceneAddress, LoadSceneMode.Additive).Task;
       Debug.Log($"Scene '{scene Address}' loaded successfully.");
     }
     catch (System.Exception ex)
     {
       Debug.LogError($"Error loading scene '{scene Address}': {ex.Message}")
     }
   }

   void OnDestroy()
   {
     // Asynchronous loading of the scene when an object is destroyed
     Addressables.UnloadSceneAsync(sceneAddress, true).Completed += handle =>
     {
       if (handle.Status == AsyncOperationStatus.Succeeded)
       {
         Debug.Log($"Scene '{sceneAddress}' was successfully unloaded.");
       }
       else
       {
```

```
                Debug.LogError($"Failed to load scene '{scene Address}'.");
            }
        };
    }
}
```

Explanation of the code:
- Using async/await makes it easier to load a scene asynchronously.
- **LoadSceneAsync** loads a scene in Additive mode, allowing it to be added to already loaded scenes.
- **UnloadSceneAsync** unloads the scene when the object is destroyed, freeing up resources.

3. Scene Setup:
   - Add a SceneLoader component to an object in the scene.
   - In the inspector, specify **sceneAddress** - the address of the scene in Addressables.

4. Load testing:
   - Run the scene and make sure the new scene loads and displays correctly.
   - Check the console for successful boot or error messages.

3.5. Script to download the font and apply it to the text

Preparing the font for Addressables

1. Import font:
   First, add the font to your project by copying it to the Assets folder. Unity automatically recognises font files such as **.ttf** and **.otf** and creates **Font** objects for them.

2. Add the font to Addressables:
   - Open **Addressables Groups** (*Window > Asset Management > Addressables > Groups*).
   - Find the imported font in the project folder, right-click and select **Mark as Addressable**.
   - Drag it to the group where you store fonts, or create a new group such as **Fonts**.

3. Set font address:
   In the font's Addressables settings, set a convenient and unique address. For example, **Fonts/MyCustomFont**. This address will be used to refer to the font in the code.

   Let's create a script that loads a font using Addressables and applies it to the UI text field. Assume that there is already a **Text** or **TextMeshPro** object on the stage.

1. Create a script: Let's call it **FontLoader.cs**.

2. Write the code to download and apply the font:

```
using UnityEngine;
using UnityEngine.UI;
using UnityEngine.AddressableAssets;
using UnityEngine.ResourceManagement.AsyncOperations;
```

```csharp
public class FontLoader : MonoBehaviour
{
    // Field for storing a link to a text UI component
    public Text uiText;

    // Address the font in Addressables
    [SerializeField]
    private string fontAddress = "Fonts/MyCustomFont";

    private void Start()
    {
        LoadAndApplyFont();
    }

    private void LoadAndApplyFont()
    {
        // Start asynchronous font loading at address
        Addressables.LoadAssetAsync<Font>(fontAddress).Completed += OnFontLoaded;
    }

    private void OnFontLoaded(AsyncOperationHandle<Font> handle)
    {
        if (handle.Status == AsyncOperationStatus.Succeeded)
        {
            Font loadedFont = handle.Result;

            // Check if there is a Text component and apply the font
            if (uiText != null)
            {
                uiText.font = loadedFont;
                Debug.Log("The font was successfully loaded and applied to the text.");
            }
        }
        else
        {
            Debug.LogError("Failed to load font from Addressables: "
                + handle.OperationException);
        }
    }

    private void OnDestroy()
    {
        // Be sure to release the resource when it is no longer needed
        Addressables.Release(handle);
    }}
```

Explanation of the code:
- **fontAddress**: The address of the font that corresponds to the Addressables setting (e.g. **Fonts/MyCustomFont**).
- **LoadAndApplyFont()**: Starts asynchronous font download at the specified address.
- **OnFontLoaded()**: Load Handler. If the font is loaded successfully, it is applied to uiText. If the download fails, a message is output to the console.
- **OnDestroy()**: Frees up a resource when it is no longer needed. This is important for memory management, especially when dynamically loading large resources.

This task can be realised via **Unitask** as follows:

```
private void Start()
  {
    // Running an asynchronous task with UniTask
    LoadAndApplyFontAsync().Forget();
  }

  private async UniTaskVoid LoadAndApplyFontAsync()
  {
    try
    {
      // Asynchronously load the font from Addressables
      loadedFont = await Addressables
          .LoadAssetAsync<Font>(fontAddress).ToUniTask();

      // If the loading was successful, apply the font to the text
      if (uiText != null && loadedFont != null)
      {
        uiText.font = loadedFont;
        Debug.Log("The font was successfully loaded and applied to the text.");
      }
    }
    catch (System.Exception e)
    {
      Debug.LogError($"Error loading font: {e.Message}");
    }
  }
```

Conclusion of the section

In this section, we looked at several practical examples of using Addressables in Unity, including loading sprites, 3D models, audio, scenes, and downloading resources from a remote server. These examples demonstrate how Addressables can be integrated into various aspects of development, improving the performance and manageability of a project. In the following sections we will delve into additional Addressables features such as optimising memory usage, managing profiles and caching strategies.

Section 4: Addressables in mobile games

Mobile platforms place special demands on optimising resource usage due to the limited capabilities of devices, such as limited RAM, limited storage and the need to save traffic when downloading data. Addressables provides powerful tools for efficient resource management in mobile applications and games. In this section, we will look at the main aspects of using Addressables on mobile platforms.

4.1. Optimising memory usage

Efficient memory management is critical for mobile applications to prevent crashes and ensure stable game performance. Addressables helps you optimise memory usage by flexibly managing the loading and unloading of resources.

4.1.1. Downloadable resources as required

Load resources only when you really need them. This reduces RAM consumption and improves performance.

Example: Dynamic loading of textures for characters:

```
using UnityEngine;
using UnityEngine.AddressableAssets;
using UnityEngine.ResourceManagement.AsyncOperations;

public class CharacterTextureLoader : MonoBehaviour
{
    public string textureAddress; // Addressable texture
    private Renderer characterRenderer;
    private AsyncOperationHandle<Texture> textureHandle;

    void Start()
    {
        characterRenderer = GetComponent<Renderer>();
        LoadTexture();
    }

    void LoadTexture()
    {
        textureHandle = Addressables.LoadAssetAsync<Texture>(textureAddress);
        textureHandle.Completed += OnTextureLoaded;
    }

    void OnTextureLoaded(AsyncOperationHandle<Texture> handle)
```

```
    {
      if (handle.Status == AsyncOperationStatus.Succeeded)
      {

        characterRenderer.material.mainTexture = handle.Result;
        Debug.Log("The texture has been successfully loaded and applied.");
      }
      else
      {

        Debug.LogError($"Failed to load texture at: {textureAddress}");
      }
    }

  void OnDestroy()
  {
    // Unloading texture when object is destroyed
    Addressables.Release(textureHandle);
  }
}
```

Explanation of the code:

- **LoadTexture** loads a texture asynchronously and applies it to the character material.
- **Addressables.Release** frees the memory occupied by the texture when the object is destroyed.

4.1.2. Using Addressables profiles for different platforms

Create separate profiles for mobile platforms to optimise resource loading and build paths, taking into account the specifics of each platform.

Steps to set up a profile:

1. **Creating a new profile for mobile platforms:**
   - Open the window **Addressables Groups**: *Window > Asset Management > Addressables > Groups*.
   - Click on the **Profile** button and select**Manage Profiles**.
   - Create a new profile, such as Mobile.

2. **Setting profile variables:**
   Change the **BuildPath** and **LoadPath** values for the mobile profile, taking into account the specifics of the platform (e.g. using local storage or CDN to download resources).

3. **Applying a profile to Addressables Groups:**
   Select the desired groups and configure their download and build paths using variables from the mobile profile.

Advantages:

- **Build Optimisation:** Different platforms may have different requirements for resource builds.

- **Download path management:** Ability to use different sources to download resources on mobile devices.

4.2. Working with different configurations (online/offline)

Many mobile games are offline or have limited network access. Addressables allows you to flexibly manage resources based on network availability.

4.2.1. Determining network availability

Use the Unity API to determine network connectivity status and load resources accordingly.

Example: Checking the network status and selecting a download source:

```
using UnityEngine;
using UnityEngine.AddressableAssets;
using UnityEngine.ResourceManagement.AsyncOperations;

public class NetworkDependentLoader : MonoBehaviour
{
    public string localAssetAddress;
    public string remoteAssetAddress;
    private string assetToLoad;

    void Start()
    {
        // Check network availability
        if (Application.internetReachability != NetworkReachability.NotReachable)
        {
            assetToLoad = remoteAssetAddress;
            Debug.Log("The network is available. A remote resource is in use.");
        }
        else
        {
            assetToLoad = localAssetAddress;
            Debug.Log("The network is unavailable. A local resource is being used.");

        }
        LoadAsset();
    }

    void LoadAsset()
    {
        Addressables.LoadAssetAsync<GameObject>(assetToLoad)
        .Completed += OnAssetLoaded;
```

```
      }

  void OnAssetLoaded(AsyncOperationHandle<GameObject> handle)
  {
    if (handle.Status == AsyncOperationStatus.Succeeded)
    {
      Instantiate(handle.Result);
      Debug.Log("The resource was successfully loaded and instantiated.");
    }
    else
    {
      Debug.LogError($"Failed to load the resource at: {assetToLoad}");
    }
  }

  void OnDestroy()
  {
    Addressables.Release(handle);
  }
}
```

Explanation of the code:
- **Application.internetReachability** checks the availability of the network.
- Depending on the state of the network, a local or remote resource is selected for downloading.

4.2.2. Resource caching

Cache downloaded resources for quick access in the future and reduced data consumption.

Example: Caching audio files:

```
using UnityEngine;
using UnityEngine.AddressableAssets;
using UnityEngine.ResourceManagement.AsyncOperations;
using System.Collections.Generic;

public class AudioCacheManager : MonoBehaviour
{
  public string audioAddress;
  private AudioSource audioSource;
  private AsyncOperationHandle<AudioClip> audioHandle;
  private static Dictionary<string, AudioClip> audioCache = new Dictionary<string,
AudioClip>();

  void Start()
  {
```

```csharp
        audioSource = gameObject.AddComponent<AudioSource>();
        LoadAudio();
    }

    void LoadAudio()
    {
        if (audioCache.ContainsKey(audioAddress))
        {
            audioSource.clip = audioCache[audioAddress];
            audioSource.Play();
            Debug.Log("Audio loaded from cache.");
        }
        else
        {
            audioHandle = Addressables.LoadAssetAsync<AudioClip>(audioAddress);
            audioHandle.Completed += OnAudioLoaded;
        }
    }

    void OnAudioLoaded(AsyncOperationHandle<AudioClip> handle)
    {
        if (handle.Status == AsyncOperationStatus.Succeeded)
        {
            audioCache[audioAddress] = handle.Result;
            audioSource.clip = handle.Result;
            audioSource.Play();
            Debug.Log("The audio was successfully downloaded and added to the cache.");
        }
        else
        {
            Debug.LogError($"Failed to load audio at: {audioAddress}");
        }
    }

    void OnDestroy()
    {
        // Upload audio when object is destroyed
        if (audioCache.ContainsKey(audioAddress))
        {
            Addressables.Release(audioHandle);
        }
    }
}
```

Explanation of the code:
- **audioCache** stores downloaded audio files for reuse.

- When loading audio, firstly it is checked if it is in the cache and if it is, it is used, otherwise it is loaded via Addressables.

4.3. Optimisation of resource loading and unloading

Resource loading and offloading optimisation helps to reduce load times, lower memory usage and ensure smooth gameplay.

4.3.1. Batch loading of resources

Load related resources in batch to minimise the number of load operations and improve performance.

Example: Batch loading multiple sprites:

```
using UnityEngine;
using UnityEngine.AddressableAssets;
using UnityEngine.ResourceManagement.AsyncOperations;
using System.Collections.Generic;
using Cysharp.Threading.Tasks;

public class BatchSpriteLoader : MonoBehaviour
{
    public List<string> spriteAddresses;
    public List<SpriteRenderer> spriteRenderers;

    async void Start()
    {
        try
        {
            var loadTasks = new List<UniTask<Sprite>>();
            foreach (var address in spriteAddresses)
            {
                loadTasks.Add(LoadSpriteAsync(address));
            }

            var sprites = await UniTask.WhenAll(loadTasks);

            for (int i = 0; i < sprites.Length; i++)
            {
                if (i < spriteRenderers.Count)
                {
                    spriteRenderers[i].sprite = sprites[i];
                }
            }
        }
```

```
            Debug.Log("All sprites have been successfully loaded and applied.");
        }
        catch (System.Exception ex)
        {
            Debug.LogError($""Error when batch loading sprites: {ex.Message}");
        }
    }

    public async UniTask<Sprite> LoadSpriteAsync(string address)
    {
        var handle = Addressables.LoadAssetAsync<Sprite>(address);
        await handle.Task;

        if (handle.Status == AsyncOperationStatus.Succeeded)
        {
            return handle.Result;
        }
        else
        {
            throw new System.Exception($"Failed to load sprite at {address}");
        }
    }

    void OnDestroy()
    {
        // Unload all sprites when an object is destroyed
        foreach (var address in spriteAddresses)
        {
            Addressables.Release(address);
        }
    }
}
}
```

Explanation of the code:
- **BatchSpriteLoader** loads multiple sprites at the same time using UniTask.WhenAll.
- Once loaded, the sprites are applied to the appropriate **SpriteRenderer**.
- Resources are unloaded when an object is destroyed.

4.3.2. Using Asset Bundles with optimal settings

Customise Asset Bundles settings for mobile platforms to reduce their size and speed up downloads.

Tips for optimising **Asset Bundles**:
- **Compression:** Use efficient compression methods, such as LZ4 or LZMA, depending on download speed and size requirements.

- **Segmentation:** Divide Asset Bundles into logical groups to load only the packages you need.
- **Texture Optimisation:** Use suitable texture formats (e.g. ETC2 for Android or PVRTC for iOS) to reduce size and improve performance.

Example of Asset Bundles compression settings:

1. Open the window Adressierbare Gruppen: *Fenster > Anlagenverwaltung > Adressaten > Gruppen*.

2. Select the Addressables group you want to configure.

3. In the inspector, find the section**Build Settings**.

4. Set Compression to LZ4 for fast loading or LZMA for maximum compression.

5. Save the settings and run the Addressables build.

4.4. Practical tips for optimisation

4.4.1. Minimizing the number of Asset Bundles

The smaller the number of Asset Bundles, the lower the overhead of loading them. Group related resources together to reduce the number of individual Asset Bundles.

Tip: Group resources by type or by scene to ensure efficient use of Asset Bundles.

4.4.2. Use of profiles for different environments

Create separate Addressables profiles for development, test and production to manage different load and build configurations.

Example:
- **Development Profile**: Uses local paths for fast testing.
- **Production Profile**: Uses remote servers to download resources.

4.4.3. Regular inspection and testing of the assembly

Check and test the Addressables build regularly to ensure that all resources are configured correctly and loaded without errors.

Tip: Automate the process of building and testing Addressables using scripts or CI/CD systems.

4.4.4. Monitoring of resource utilisation

Use Unity's profiling tools and your own logging systems to track load and resource usage to identify and resolve bottlenecks.

Tip: Enable resource utilisation logging for real-time analysis.

4.5. Example: Optimising resource utilisation in a mobile game

Let's take a look at a comprehensive example of optimising resource utilisation in a mobile game using Addressables. We will create a system that loads the necessary resources as needed, caches them for reuse, and manages memory efficiently.

Implementation steps:

1. **Customisation Addressables Groups:**
   - Create groups for key resources such as textures, models, audio.
   - Configure groups for remote storage if dynamic content updates are required.

2. **Establishment of a resource management system:** Create a **ResourceManager.cs** script that will be responsible for loading, caching and unloading resources.

```csharp
using UnityEngine;
using UnityEngine.AddressableAssets;
using UnityEngine.ResourceManagement.AsyncOperations;
using Cysharp.Threading.Tasks;
using System.Collections.Generic;

public class ResourceManager : MonoBehaviour
{
  private static ResourceManager instance;
  private Dictionary<string, AsyncOperationHandle<Object>> resourceCache = new
Dictionary<string, AsyncOperationHandle<Object>>();

  void Awake()
  {
    if (instance == null)
    {
      instance = this;
      DontDestroyOnLoad(gameObject);
    }
    else
    {
      Destroy(gameObject);
    }
  }

  public async UniTask<T> LoadResourceAsync<T>(string address) where T : Object
  {
    if (resourceCache.ContainsKey(address))
    {
      return resourceCache[address].Result as T;
    }
```

```csharp
        else
        {
            var handle = Addressables.LoadAssetAsync<T>(address);
            await handle.Task;
            if (handle.Status == AsyncOperationStatus.Succeeded)
            {
                resourceCache[address] = handle;
                return handle.Result;
            }
            else
            {
                Debug.LogError($"Failed to load resource at: {address}");
                return null;
            }
        }
    }


    public void ReleaseResource(string address)
    {
        if (resourceCache.ContainsKey(address))
        {
            Addressables.Release(resourceCache[address]);
            resourceCache.Remove(address);
            Debug.Log($"The resource at {address} was successfully unloaded.");
        }
        else
        {
            Debug.LogWarning($"Attempt to unload a non-existent resource at: {address}");
        }
    }

    public void ReleaseAllResources()
    {
        foreach (var handle in resourceCache.Values)
        {
            Addressables.Release(handle);
        }
        resourceCache.Clear();
        Debug.Log("All resources were successfully unloaded.");
    }
}
```

Explanation of the code:
- **Singleton Pattern**: Ensures that there is a single instance of ResourceManager in the project.
- **LoadResourceAsync<T>**: Loads the resource asynchronously and caches it for reuse.

- **ReleaseResource**: Uploads a specific resource at.
- **ReleaseAllResources**: Unloads all loaded resources, freeing memory.

Using ResourceManager to load resources:

Create a **CharacterManager.cs** script that will use **ResourceManager** to load and unload 3D character models.

```
using UnityEngine;
using Cysharp.Threading.Tasks;

public class CharacterManager : MonoBehaviour
{
    public string characterModelAddress;
    private GameObject characterInstance;

    async void Start()
    {
        characterInstance = await ResourceManager.Instance
            .LoadResourceAsync<GameObject>(characterModelAddress);

        if (characterInstance != null)
        {
            Instantiate(characterInstance, Vector3.zero, Quaternion.identity);
            Debug.Log("The character was successfully loaded and instantiated.");
        }
    }

    void OnDestroy()
    {
        if (characterInstance != null)
        {
            ResourceManager.Instance.ReleaseResource(characterModelAddress);
            Destroy(characterInstance);
            Debug.Log("The character has been unloaded and deleted.");
        }
    }
}
```

1. Explanation of the code:
   - **LoadResourceAsync<GameObject>** loads a 3D model of the character.
   - **Instantiate** creates an instance of the loaded character in the scene.
   - **ReleaseResource** unloads the model when the object is destroyed, freeing memory.

2. Testing and profiling:
   - **Test** loading and unloading resources on different mobile devices.
   - Use **Unity Profiler** to track memory usage and performance.
   - **Optimise** Asset Bundles and Addressables settings based on your findings.

4.6. Management of loading and unloading depending on usage scenarios

Different game scenarios may require different approaches to loading and unloading resources. Addressables allows you to flexibly customise these processes depending on the needs of your project.

4.6.1. Loading resources when entering a scene

When moving to a new scene, load resources required for that scene and unload resources not required in the current scene.

Example: Automatic loading of resources when loading a scene:

```
using UnityEngine;
using UnityEngine.AddressableAssets;
using UnityEngine.ResourceManagement.AsyncOperations;
using Cysharp.Threading.Tasks;

public class SceneResourceManager : MonoBehaviour
{
    public string sceneAddress;
    public string[] requiredResourceAddresses;

    async void Start()
    {
        // Loading the scene
        await Addressables.LoadSceneAsync(sceneAddress,
            UnityEngine.SceneManagement
            .LoadSceneMode.Additive).Task;
        Debug.Log($"Scene '{scene Address}' loaded successfully.");

        // Loading required resources
        foreach (var address in requiredResourceAddresses)
        {
            var resource = await ResourceManager.Instance
            .LoadResourceAsync<GameObject>(address);

            if (resource != null)
            {
                Instantiate(resource);
                Debug.Log($"Resource '{address}' has been loaded and instantiated.");
            }
        }
    }

    void OnDestroy()
    {
        // Unload resources and scenes when an object is destroyed
        foreach (var address in requiredResourceAddresses)
```

```
      {
         ResourceManager.Instance.ReleaseResource(address);
      }

      Addressables.UnloadSceneAsync(sceneAddress).Completed += handle =>
      {
         if (handle.Status == AsyncOperationStatus.Succeeded)
         {
            Debug.Log($"Scene '{sceneAddress}' uploaded successfully.");
         }
         else
         {
            Debug.LogError($"Failed to unload scene '{sceneAddress}'.");
         }
      };
   }
}
}
```

Explanation of the code:
- **LoadSceneAsync** loads the scene in Additive mode.
- **LoadResourceAsync<GameObject>** loads the required resources and instantiates them in the scene.
- **ReleaseResource** and **UnloadSceneAsync** unload resources and the scene when the object is destroyed.

4.6.2. Lazy loading

Lazy loading implies loading resources only when they are first used, not in advance. This helps to reduce the initial boot time and distribute the load of loading resources.

Example: Lazy loading of a game object when using it for the first time:

```
using UnityEngine;
using Cysharp.Threading.Tasks;

public class LazyLoadObject : MonoBehaviour
{
   public string objectAddress;
   private GameObject loadedObject;
   private bool isLoaded = false;

   void OnMouseDown()
   {
      if (!isLoaded)
      {
         LoadObject().Forget();
      }
```

```csharp
      else
      {
        ToggleObjectVisibility();
      }
  }

  private async UniTaskVoid LoadObject()
  {
    try
    {
      loadedObject = await ResourceManager.Instance
           .LoadResourceAsync<GameObject>(objectAddress);
      if (loadedObject != null)
      {
        loadedObject = Instantiate(loadedObject, transform.position
         + Vector3.up * 2, Quaternion.identity);
        isLoaded = true;
        Debug.Log("The object was successfully loaded and instantiated.");
      }
    }
    catch (System.Exception ex)
    {
      Debug.LogError($"Error loading object: {ex.Message}");
    }
  }

  private void ToggleObjectVisibility()
  {
    if (loadedObject != null)
    {
      loadedObject.SetActive(!loadedObject.activeSelf);
      Debug.Log($"Object is now {(loaded Object.activeSelf ? "active" : "not active")}.");
    }
  }

  void OnDestroy()
  {
    if (loadedObject != null)
    {
      ResourceManager.Instance.ReleaseResource(objectAddress);
      Destroy(loadedObject);
      Debug.Log("Object unloaded and deleted.");
    }
  }
}
```

Explanation of the code:
- **OnMouseDown**: When you click on an object, it checks if the resource is loaded. If not, loads it.
- **LoadObject**: Asynchronously loads and instantiates an object.
- **ToggleObjectVisibility**: Switches the visibility of the loaded object when you click again.
- **ReleaseResource**: Unloads the resource when the object is destroyed.

4.6.3. Load priority management

Manage resource loading priorities so that important resources are loaded first, providing quick access to key elements of the game.

Example: Loading interface sprites with high priority:

```
using UnityEngine;
using UnityEngine.AddressableAssets;
using UnityEngine.ResourceManagement.AsyncOperations;
using Cysharp.Threading.Tasks;

public class HighPriorityLoader : MonoBehaviour
{
    public string highPrioritySpriteAddress;
    public string lowPrioritySpriteAddress;

    async void Start()
    {
        // Load high priority sprite
        var highPriorityTask = LoadAssetAsync<Sprite>(highPrioritySpriteAddress,
            priority: 1);

        // Load low priority sprite
        var lowPriorityTask = LoadAssetAsync<Sprite>(lowPrioritySpriteAddress, priority: 0);
        await UniTask.WhenAll(highPriorityTask, lowPriorityTask);
        Debug.Log("All sprites are loaded based on priority.");
    }

    public async UniTask<Sprite> LoadAssetAsync<T>(string address, int priority = 0)
        where T : Object
    {
        var handle = Addressables.LoadAssetAsync<T>(address);
        handle.Priority = priority;

        // Set download priority
        await handle.Task;
        if (handle.Status == AsyncOperationStatus.Succeeded)
        {
            return handle.Result as Sprite;
        }
    }
```

```
      else
      {
        throw new System.Exception($"Failed to load resource at {address}");
      }
  }

  void OnDestroy()
  {
      // Unload resources when an object is destroyed
      Addressables.Release(highPrioritySpriteAddress);
      Addressables.Release(lowPrioritySpriteAddress);
  }
}
```

Explanation of the code:
- **handle.Priority** sets the download priority of the resource. A high priority (higher number) means that the resource will be loaded faster.
- **UniTask.WhenAll** allows you to load several resources at the same time, taking into account their priorities.

Conclusion of the section

In this section, we looked at how to use Addressables effectively in mobile games, focusing on optimising memory usage, managing resource loading and unloading, dealing with different configurations, and managing load priorities. These approaches will help you create mobile apps and games with high performance and stability, while providing a better user experience.

Recommendations and advice

1. Plan your Addressables structure in advance: Well-organised Addressables groups make resource management and optimisation easier.

2. Use profiles for different environments and platforms: This will allow you to flexibly customise the paths for loading and building resources.

3. Test on target devices: Optimisation can vary greatly from device to device, so regular testing is important to identify and fix problems.

4. Monitor memory usage: Use Unity Profiler and other tools to monitor memory usage and performance.

5. Document your settings: Maintaining documentation of Addressables settings will help in maintaining and developing the project, especially in teamwork.

Section 5: Additional Addressables Features

Addressables provides not only basic resource management tools, but also a number of advanced features that allow developers to more flexibly and efficiently manage content in their projects. In this section, we will cover the following topics:

1. Working with profiles and configurations for different platforms

2. Allocation of resources to AssetBundles

3. Caching and resource reuse strategies

4. Use of scripts and process automation

5. Integrating Addressables with other systems

6. Advanced Optimisation Techniques

5.1. Working with profiles and configurations for different platforms

Addressables profiles allow you to create different build and resource loading configurations for different platforms or development environments (e.g. development, testing, production). This is especially useful when you want to use different load paths or different sets of resources depending on the environment.

Steps for working with profiles:

1. **Creating a new profile:**

   - Open the window **Addressables Groups**: *Window > Asset Management > Addressables > Groups*.

   - Click **Profile** (usually represented by a gear icon) and select **Manage Profiles**.

   - In the window **Manage Profiles** click **Add** and enter a name for the new profile, e.g. Production or Development.

2. **Setting profile variables:**

   - Each profile contains a set of variables such as BuildPath, LoadPath, RemoteBuildPath and RemoteLoadPath.

   - Change the values of these variables to suit the requirements of your platform or environment.

   - For example, for the Production profile, you can set RemoteLoadPath to the URL of your CDN, and use local paths for Development.

3. **Applying the profile to groups:**

- Select the desired group in the window **Addressables Groups**.

- In the inspector, find the section **Build and Load Paths**.

- Replace the current paths with the appropriate profile variables using the syntax ${VariableName}.

- For example, replace the download path with ${RemoteLoadPath}.

4. **Switching between profiles:**

- In the **Manage Profiles** window, select the desired profile from the drop-down list.

- All groups using this profile's variables will automatically update their download and build paths.

Example of using profiles:

```
using UnityEngine;
using UnityEngine.AddressableAssets;

public class ProfileManager : MonoBehaviour
{
  void Start()
  {
    // Get the current profile
    var currentProfile = Addressables.RuntimePath;
    Debug.Log("Current download path: " + currentProfile);
    // Example of changing profile (you need to restart the application)
    // Addressables.SetCurrentProfile("Production");
  }
}
```

Explanation of the code:
- Addressables.RuntimePath returns the current boot path based on the active profile.
- The **SetCurrentProfile** method allows you to change the profile, but requires restarting the application to apply the changes.

5.2. Allocation of resources to AssetBundles

AssetBundles — are packages containing one or more resources that can be loaded and unloaded dynamically. Addressables automatically manages the creation and distribution of AssetBundles, but the developer can control this process in more detail to optimise the process.

Steps for resource allocation:

1. **Resource grouping:**

   - Organise your resources into logical groups in the window **Addressables Groups**.

   - For example, create separate groups for textures, models, audio, etc.

2. **Configuring the group settings:**

   Select the group and in the inspector configure the build parameters:

   - **Bundle Mode**: defines how resources will be packed into AssetBundles. Options:

   - **Pack Separately**: each resource is packed into a separate AssetBundle.

   - **Pack Together**: all resources of the group are packed into one AssetBundle.

   - **Pack by Label**: resources with the same label are packaged together.

   - **Compression**: select compression method (e.g. LZ4 for fast loading or LZMA for maximum compression).

3. **Dependency creation:**

   - Addressables automatically detects dependencies between resources and includes them in the appropriate AssetBundles.

   - You can manually manage dependencies to optimise your downloads.

4. **Assembly AssetBundles:**

   - In the **Addressables Groups** window, click **Build > New Build > Default Build Script**.

   - Unity will create AssetBundles according to the group settings.

Example of resource allocation:

```
using UnityEngine;
using UnityEngine.AddressableAssets;
using UnityEngine.ResourceManagement.AsyncOperations;

public class AssetBundleLoader : MonoBehaviour
{
  public string assetBundleAddress;

  void Start()
  {
    // Asynchronous loading AssetBundle
    Addressables.LoadAssetAsync<GameObject>(assetBundleAddress)
    .Completed += OnAssetLoaded;
  }

  void OnAssetLoaded(AsyncOperationHandle<GameObject> handle)
  {
```

```
        if (handle.Status == AsyncOperationStatus.Succeeded)
        {
            // Instantiate the loaded object
            Instantiate(handle.Result);
            Debug.Log("AssetBundle was successfully loaded and the object was instantiated.");

        }
        else
        {
            Debug.LogError($"Failed to load AssetBundle at: {assetBundleAddress}");
        }
    }

    void OnDestroy()
    {
        // Unload AssetBundle when object is destroyed
        Addressables.Release(handle);
    }
}
```

Explanation of the code:
- **assetBundleAddress** — the address of the AssetBundle to be loaded.
- **LoadAssetAsync<GameObject>** — method to load an object from AssetBundle.
- **Instantiate** creates an instance of the loaded object in the scene.
- **Release** frees the memory occupied by AssetBundle.

5.3. Caching and resource reuse strategies

Caching allows you to save downloaded resources for reuse without having to re-download them. This reduces download time and saves traffic, especially when working with remote resources.

Steps to implement caching:

1. **Enabling caching:**
   - Addressables automatically caches the uploaded **AssetBundles**.
   - To manage the cache, you can use the class **Caching**.

2. **Configuring caching settings:**
   - You can set the maximum cache size and manage cache clearing.

Example of cache configuration:

```
using UnityEngine;

public class CacheManager : MonoBehaviour
{
```

```
void Start()
{
  // Set the maximum cache size (for example, 500 MB)
  Caching.maximumAvailableDiskSpace = 500 * 1024 * 1024;

  // Check available cache space
  long availableSpace = Caching.currentDiskUsage;
  Debug.Log("Current cache usage: " + available Space + " bytes");
}

public void ClearCache()
{
  // Clear all cache
  Caching.ClearCache();
  Debug.Log("Cache cleared.");
}
}
```

Explanation of the code:
- **Caching.maximumAvailableDiskSpace** sets the maximum available cache space.
- **Caching.ClearCache()** clears all cache.

How Addressables work with Caching
1. **Autocaching:**

   - When you upload a resource via Addressables.LoadAssetAsync, if it is downloaded from remote storage, Addressables uses UnityWebRequest, which automatically saves the uploaded file to Unity Caching.
   - If the resource is already in the cache (and its version matches), Unity uses the cache instead of downloading it.

2. **Version Definition:**

   - Each Addressable resource has a version that is stored in the Content Catalog.
   - If the version of the resource in the cache matches the version in the catalogue, the download is from the cache.

3. **Cache management:**

   - Addressables automatically add data to the cache and retrieve it from there.
   - If you need to disable the cache or force reloading of resources, this needs to be configured manually.

How Addressables put resources in the cache
Addressables use the UnityWebRequest system to load resources. If you are using:

- Addressables.DownloadDependenciesAsync: Resources are downloaded and automatically saved to Unity Caching.
- Addressables.LoadAssetAsync: If the resource is already cached, it is loaded from the cache.

To add resources to the cache, simply useDownloadDependenciesAsync.

Reusing resources from the cache:

- Addressables automatically checks for resources in the cache before downloading them from the server.
- You can manually manage the downloading of resources from the cache or updating them.

5.4. Use of scripts and process automation

Automation of Addressables assembly and control processes saves time and reduces the chance of manual set-up errors. Using scripts (scripts) for automation can significantly improve the development workflow.

Steps to automate the Addressables build:

1. Creating an editorial script to build Addressables:

```
using UnityEditor;
using UnityEditor.AddressableAssets;
using UnityEditor.AddressableAssets.Settings;

public class AddressablesBuilder
{
  [MenuItem("Tools/Build Addressables")]
  public static void BuildAddressables()
  {
    AddressableAssetSettings settings = AddressableAssetSettingsDefaultObject.Settings;
    if (settings == null)
    {
     UnityEngine.Debug.LogError("AddressableAssetSettings not found.
         Make sure Addressables are configured.");
      return;
    }
    AddressableAssetSettings.BuildPlayerContent();
    UnityEngine.Debug.Log("Addressables were successfully collected.");
  }
}
```

Explanation of the code:
- MenuItem adds a new item to the Unity menu calledTools/Build Addressables.
- The BuildAddressables method initiates the building of Addressables via theBuildPlayerContent().

2. Use of the script:
- In Unity, open the Tools menu and select Build Addressables.

- The script will automatically build Addressables according to the current group and profile settings.

3. Extension of scenarios:
- You can add additional steps to the script, such as uploading collected AssetBundles to the server or sending notifications after a successful build.

Example of an extended scenario:

```
using UnityEditor;
using UnityEditor.AddressableAssets;
using UnityEditor.AddressableAssets.Settings;
using System.Diagnostics;

public class ExtendedAddressablesBuilder
{
  [MenuItem("Tools/Build and Upload Addressables")]
  public static void BuildAndUploadAddressables()
  {
    AddressableAssetSettings settings = AddressableAssetSettingsDefaultObject.Settings;
    if (settings == null)
    {
      UnityEngine.Debug.LogError("AddressableAssetSettings not found. Make sure
        Addressables are configured.");
      return;
    }
    // Build Addressables
    AddressableAssetSettings.BuildPlayerContent();
    UnityEngine.Debug.Log("Addressables were successfully collected.");

    // Upload to the server (example of using an external script)
    Process.Start("upload_script.bat");
    UnityEngine.Debug.Log("The server upload script has started.");
  }
}
```

Explanation of the code:
- After building Addressables, an external script upload_script.bat is run to upload AssetBundles to the server.
- This allows you to automate the entire process of building and deploying resources.

Benefits of automation:
- **Time saving:** Reduced time for manual operations.
- **Reduced errors:** Less chance of errors during manual adjustment.
- **Increasing consistency:** Uniform assembly and deposition processes.

5.5. Integrating Addressables with other systems

Addressables can be integrated with various systems and libraries to extend functionality and improve workflow.

5.5.1. Integration with version control systems

Use version control systems (such as Git) to track changes to Addressables and AssetBundles settings.

Tips:

Ignore cache and temporary files: Add appropriate rules to .gitignore to keep cached AssetBundles and temporary files out of the repository.

```
# Ignore Addressables cache

Library/com.unity.addressables/
```

Track Addressables settings: Include Addressables settings files (AddressableAssetSettings.asset) in the version control system for team collaboration.

5.5.2. Integration with CI/CD systems

Automate Addressables build and deploy processes with CI/CD systems such as Jenkins, GitHub Actions or GitLab CI.

Example: Configuring GitHub Actions to build Addressables**:**

Create a **workflow file**: .github/workflows/build_addressables.yml

```
name: Build Addressables

on:
  push:
    branches:
      - main

jobs:
  build:
    runs-on: ubuntu-latest

    steps:
      - uses: actions/checkout@v2

      - name: Set up Unity
```

```
    uses: game-ci/unity-builder@v2
    with:
     unityVersion: 2021.3.0f1

   - name: Build Addressables
    run: |
     unity -batchmode -quit -projectPath . -executeMethod
AddressablesBuilder.BuildAddressables -logFile
```

Explanation:
- Each time you push into the main branch, a job runs that installs Unity and executes the BuildAddressables method from your editorial script.

5.5.3. Integration with analytics systems

Track resource usage and user behaviour using analytics systems such as Unity Analytics or third-party services.

Example: Sending analytics events when resources are loaded:

```csharp
using UnityEngine;
using UnityEngine.AddressableAssets;
using UnityEngine.ResourceManagement.AsyncOperations;
using UnityEngine.Analytics;
using System.Collections.Generic;

public class AnalyticsResourceLoader : MonoBehaviour
{
  public string resourceAddress;

  void Start()
  {
    Addressables.LoadAssetAsync<GameObject>(resourceAddress)
      .Completed += OnResourceLoaded;
  }

  void OnResourceLoaded(AsyncOperationHandle<GameObject> handle)
  {
    if (handle.Status == AsyncOperationStatus.Succeeded)
    {
      Instantiate(handle.Result);
      UnityEngine.Debug.Log("The server upload script has started.");

      // Send analytics event
      Analytics.CustomEvent("ResourceLoaded", new Dictionary<string, object>
      {
```

```
            { "Address", resourceAddress },
            { "Timestamp", System.DateTime.UtcNow }
        });
    }
    else
    {

        Debug.Log Error($"Failed to load resource at: {resource Address}");
        // Send an error event
        Analytics.CustomEvent("ResourceLoadFailed", new Dictionary<string, object>
        {
            { "Address", resourceAddress },
            { "Timestamp", System.DateTime.UtcNow }
        });
    }
  }

  void OnDestroy()
  {
    Addressables.Release(handle);
  }
}
```

Explanation of the code:
- Once the resource is loaded, user events are sent to the analytics system.
- This allows you to track successful and unsuccessful downloads of resources, as well as analyse user behaviour.

5.6. Advanced Optimisation Techniques

To maximise the efficiency of Addressables, various advanced optimisation techniques can be applied to reduce load times, reduce the size of AssetBundles and improve application performance.

5.6.1. Optimization AssetBundles

- **Splitting large AssetBundles:** Avoid creating AssetBundles that are too large, which can slow down loading. Split them into smaller bundles corresponding to logical resource groups.
  Example:
    Create separate AssetBundles for textures, models, and audio to load only the necessary packages as needed.
- **Using the right texture formats:** Choose the best texture formats for your target platforms (e.g. ETC2 for Android or PVRTC for iOS) to reduce size and improve performance.
  Tip:
    In the texture import settings, select the appropriate format and adjust the compression settings.

5.6.2. Asynchronous uploading of resources

Efficiently offload resources when they are no longer needed to free up memory and improve performance.

Example: Automatic unloading of resources after use:

```
using UnityEngine;
using UnityEngine.AddressableAssets;
using UnityEngine.ResourceManagement.AsyncOperations;

public class AutoUnloadResource : MonoBehaviour
{
    public string resourceAddress;
    private AsyncOperationHandle<GameObject> handle;
    private GameObject instance;

    void Start()
    {
        handle = Addressables.LoadAssetAsync<GameObject>(resourceAddress);
        handle.Completed += OnResourceLoaded;
    }

    void OnResourceLoaded(AsyncOperationHandle<GameObject> handle)
    {
        if (handle.Status == AsyncOperationStatus.Succeeded)
        {
            instance = Instantiate(handle.Result);
            Debug.Log("The resource has been loaded and instantiated.");
            // Schedule an upload after a certain time or event
            // Unload after 10 seconds
            Invoke(nameof(UnloadResource), 10f);
            Debug.Log("The resource has been loaded and instantiated.");
            // Schedule unloading after a certain time
                or event Invoke(nameof(UnloadResource), 10f);
        }
        else
        {
            Debug.Log Error($"Failed to load resource at: {resource Address}");
        }
    }

    void UnloadResource()
    {
        if (instance != null)
        {
```

```
      Destroy(instance);
    }
    Addressables.Release(handle);
    Debug.Log("The resource has been unloaded from memory.");
  }

  void OnDestroy()
  {
    // Ensure unloading when object is destroyed
    if (instance != null)
    {
      Destroy(instance);
    }
    Addressables.Release(handle);
  }
}
```

Explanation of the code:
- The resource is loaded and instantiated.
- After 10 seconds, the resource is automatically uploaded.
- This allows for efficient memory management, especially in large projects.

5.6.3. Using preloading (Preloading)

Preloading resources that are likely to be needed in the near future can improve the user experience by reducing latency when using them.

Example: Preloading resources when loading a scene:

```
using UnityEngine;
using UnityEngine.AddressableAssets;
using UnityEngine.ResourceManagement.AsyncOperations;
using Cysharp.Threading.Tasks;
using System.Collections.Generic;

public class Preloader : MonoBehaviour
{
  public List<string> resourcesToPreload;

  async void Start()
  {
    await PreloadResources();
    Debug.Log("Resource preload completed.");
  }
```

```
public async UniTask PreloadResources()
{
    var preloadTasks = new List<UniTask>();

    foreach (var address in resourcesToPreload)
    {
        preloadTasks.Add(Addressables.LoadAssetAsync<Object>(address)
          .Task.ToUniTask());
    }
    await UniTask.WhenAll(preloadTasks);
}

void OnDestroy()
{
    // Unloading preloaded resources
    foreach (var address in resourcesToPreload)
    {
        Addressables.Release(address);
    }
}
}
```

Explanation of the code:
- **resourcesToPreload** — list of resource addresses to be preloaded.
- **PreloadResources** loads all the specified resources asynchronously.
- Pre-loaded resources will be available instantly when you continue to use them.

Conclusion of the section

In this section, we looked at the advanced features of Addressables, including working with profiles and configurations for different platforms, allocating resources to AssetBundles, caching and resource reuse strategies, using scripts to automate processes, integrating Addressables with other systems, and advanced optimisation techniques. These tools and approaches allow you to maximise the use of Addressables in your Unity projects, improving the performance, manageability and flexibility of your content.

Recommendations and advice

1. **Dig deep into the documentation:** Unity provides extensive documentation on Addressables. Refer to it regularly to understand new features and best practices.

2. **Experiment with settings:** Try different group and profile settings to find the best configuration for your project.

3. **Use profiling tools:** Unity Profiler and other tools can help you monitor resource usage and identify performance bottlenecks.

4. **Document your processes:** Keeping detailed documentation of Addressables settings and processes will make it easier to support your project and work as a team.

5. **Stay tuned:** Unity is constantly updating Addressables with new features and improvements. Keep your project up to date.

6. **Learn from examples:** Explore project examples and scenarios using Addressables to adopt best practices and solve challenges that arise.

Section 6: Errors and their resolution

Working with Addressables in Unity offers many benefits, but like any other tool, it can cause some difficulties and errors. In this section, we'll look at the most common problems developers may encounter and offer step-by-step solutions for troubleshooting them.

6.1. Error:"Addressables is not initialized."

Problem Description:

This error occurs when an attempt to load an Addressable resource is made before the Addressables system is fully initialised. This can happen if a script attempts to load a resource in the Awake() method or too early in an object's lifecycle.

Decision:

Ensure that Addressables are initialised before loading resources. The best place for initialisation is the Start().

Example of misuse:

```
using UnityEngine;
using UnityEngine.AddressableAssets;

public class EarlyLoader : MonoBehaviour
{
  void Awake()
  {
    Addressables.LoadAssetAsync<GameObject>("MyPrefab")
      .Completed += OnLoadDone;
  }
  void OnLoadDone(UnityEngine.ResourceManagement.AsyncOperations
      .AsyncOperationHandle<GameObject> handle)
  {
    // Process loading
  }
}
```

Corrected example:

```
using UnityEngine;
using UnityEngine.AddressableAssets;

public class CorrectLoader : MonoBehaviour
{
```

```
void Start()
{
  Addressables.LoadAssetAsync<GameObject>("MyPrefab")
    .Completed += OnLoadDone;
}

void OnLoadDone(UnityEngine.ResourceManagement
    .AsyncOperations.AsyncOperationHandle<GameObject> handle)
{
   // Process loading
}
}
```

Additional recommendations:
- Use the Start() method instead of Awake() to initialise Addressables.
- Ensure that Addressables Groups are correctly configured and initialised before use.

6.2. Error: "Failed to load asset at address."

Problem Description:

This error indicates that Addressables could not find or load the resource at the specified address. Possible causes include:
- Incorrect resource address.
- The resource has not been labelled asAddressable.
- Problems with AssetBundles or loading them.

Decision:

1. **Check the address of the resource:**

   - Ensure that the address specified in the script matches exactly the address assigned to the resource in Addressables Groups.
   - Pay attention to the case of letters and the absence of extra spaces.

2. **Ensure that the resource is marked as Addressable:**

   - In **Project Window**, check that the resource has a tick in the **Addressable** box.
   - Rebuild Addressables after adding or modifying resources.

3. **Check the assembly Addressables:**

   - Make sure AssetBundles are correctly built and available for downloading.
   - Go to *Window > Asset Management > Addressables > Groups* and press *Build > New Build > Default Build Script*.

Address verification example:

```
using UnityEngine;
using UnityEngine.AddressableAssets;

public class AssetLoader : MonoBehaviour
{
    public string correctAddress = "MyPrefab";
    public string incorrectAddress = "MyPrefabWrong";

    void Start()
    {
        // Attempt to download with the correct address
        Addressables.LoadAssetAsync<GameObject>(correctAddress)
            .Completed += OnLoadDone;
        // Attempted to download from an incorrect address (will throw an error)
        Addressables.LoadAssetAsync<GameObject>(incorrectAddress)
            .Completed += OnLoadDone;
    }

    void OnLoadDone(UnityEngine.ResourceManagement
        .AsyncOperations.AsyncOperationHandle<GameObject> handle)
    {
        if (handle.Status == UnityEngine.ResourceManagement.AsyncOperations
            .AsyncOperationStatus.Succeeded)
        {
            Instantiate(handle.Result);
            Debug.Log("Resource loaded successfully.");
        }
        else
        {
            Debug.LogError("Failed to load resource.");
        }
    }
}
```

Additional recommendations:
- Use unique and descriptive addresses for resources to avoid confusion.
- Regularly update and rebuild Addressables after making changes to resources.

6.3. Error: "Failed to download catalog."

Problem Description:

This error occurs when attempting to load the Addressables directory, especially when using remote resources. Causes may include:

- Incorrect URL to load the catalogue.

- Problems accessing the server or network.

- Catalogue version mismatch.

Decision:

1. **Check the URL to download the catalogue:**
   - Ensure that **RemoteLoadPath** is configured correctly in the Addressables profiles.
   - Check URL availability via browser or HTTP request testing tools.

2. **Check the network connection:**
   - Make sure your device has access to the internet.
   - Check your firewall and proxy settings, if applicable.

3. **Synchronisation of catalogue versions:**
   - Make sure that the local and remote directory versions are the same.
   - When updating Addressables, be sure to update both the local and remote directories.

Example of remote directory configuration:

```
using UnityEngine;
using UnityEngine.AddressableAssets;
using UnityEngine.ResourceManagement.AsyncOperations;
using Cysharp.Threading.Tasks;

public class CatalogLoader : MonoBehaviour
{
    async void Start()
    {
        try
        {
            // Check for catalog updates
            var updateResult = await Addressables.CheckForCatalogUpdates().Task;
            if (updateResult.Count > 0)
            {
                // Update directory
                await Addressables.UpdateCatalogs(updateResult).Task;
                Debug.Log("Directory updated successfully.");
            }
            else
```

```
        {
            Debug.Log("No catalog updates found.");
        }
    }
    catch (System.Exception ex)
    {
        Debug.LogError($"Error loading directory: {ex.Message}");
    }
  }
}
}
```

Additional recommendations:
- Use mechanisms to retry to load the catalogue in case of temporary network failures.
- Log detailed error information to simplify diagnostics.

6.4. Error: "AssetBundles have not been built."

Problem Description:

This error occurs when Addressables attempt to load resources but the corresponding AssetBundles have not yet been collected. This can happen after adding new resources or changing Addressables group settings.

Decision:

1. **Collect AssetBundles:**

   - Go to *Window > Asset Management > Addressables > Groups*.

   - Press *Build > New Build > Default Build Script*.

2. **Check the groups Addressables:**

   - Ensure that all required groups contain the right resources and are configured correctly.

   - Check that the resources have unique addresses and are correctly assigned to groups.

3. **Check the assembly settings:**

   - Make sure that the correct build and download paths are selected in the Addressables settings.

Example of AssetBundles validation and build:

```
using UnityEditor;
using UnityEditor.AddressableAssets.Settings;

public class AddressablesBuilder
```

```
{
  [MenuItem("Tools/Build Addressables")]
  public static void BuildAddressables()
  {
    AddressableAssetSettings settings = AddressableAssetSettingsDefaultObject.Settings;
    if (settings == null)
    {
      Debug.LogError("AddressableAssetSettings not found. Make sure Addressables are
configured.");
      return;
    }
    AddressableAssetSettings.BuildPlayerContent();
    Debug.LogError("AddressableAssetSettings not found. Make sure Addressables are
configured.");
  }
}
```

Additional recommendations:
- Automate the Addressables build process with editorial scripts and CI/CD systems.
- Regularly rebuild Addressables after making changes to the project.

6.5. Error: "Insufficient memory to load AssetBundle."

Problem Description:

This error occurs when the device does not have enough RAM to load and instantiate the AssetBundle. This is especially true for mobile devices with limited resources.

Decision:

1. **Optimise sizes AssetBundles:**

   a. Reduce the size of resources within AssetBundles using optimal formats and levels of detail.
   b. Split large AssetBundles into smaller ones to load only the necessary parts.

2. **Use Addressables.Release:**

   a. Make sure you release resources after they are used by calling Addressables.Release or Addressables.ReleaseInstance.

3. **Optimize memory:**

   a. Avoid loading a large number of resources at the same time.
   b. Use Unity profiling techniques to monitor memory usage and identify leaks.

Example of releasing resources after use:

```csharp
using UnityEngine;
using UnityEngine.AddressableAssets;
using UnityEngine.ResourceManagement.AsyncOperations;

public class MemoryOptimizedLoader : MonoBehaviour
{
    public string prefabAddress;
    private AsyncOperationHandle<GameObject> handle;
    private GameObject instance;

    void Start()
    {
        LoadPrefab();
    }

    void LoadPrefab()
    {
        handle = Addressables.LoadAssetAsync<GameObject>(prefabAddress);
        handle.Completed += OnPrefabLoaded;
    }

    void OnPrefabLoaded(AsyncOperationHandle<GameObject> handle)
    {
        if (handle.Status == AsyncOperationStatus.Succeeded)
        {
            instance = Instantiate(handle.Result);
            Debug.Log("Prefab successfully loaded and instantiated.");
        }
        else
        {
            Debug.Log Error($"Failed to load prefab at: {prefab Address}");
        }
    }

    void OnDestroy()
    {
        if (instance != null)
        {
            Destroy(instance);
        }
        Addressables.Release(handle);
        Debug.Log Error($"Failed to load prefab at: {prefab Address}");
    }
}
```

Additional recommendations:
- Use Unity profiler to identify and fix memory leaks.
- Optimise the loading and unloading of resources according to the needs of the game.

6.6. Error: "Circular dependency detected."

Problem Description:

This error occurs when there is a cyclic dependency between resources in Addressables. For example, AssetBundle A depends on AssetBundle B, and AssetBundle B depends on AssetBundle A. Such dependencies can lead to endless load cycles and failures.

Decision:

1. **Identify cyclic dependencies:**

   - Use Addressables dependency analysis tools or third-party utilities to identify loops.

2. **Rebuild your dependency architecture:**

   - Divide resources in a way that avoids cyclic dependencies.
   - Use generic AssetBundles for resources that other bundles depend on.

3. **Check dependencies before assembly:**

   - Before running the Addressables build, make sure that all dependencies are configured correctly and that there are no loops.

Example of avoiding cyclic dependencies:

```
// Let's say you have two prefabs: Enemy and Weapon.
// Enemy depends on Weapon, but Weapon should not depend on Enemy.

// In Addressables Groups:
- Create a separate "Weapons" group for Weapon prefabs.
- Create a group "Enemies" for Enemy prefabs that depend on Weapon.
- Make sure the "Weapons" group is not dependent on "Enemies".
```

Additional recommendations:
- Plan the structure of Addressables groups in advance to minimise the risk of cyclical dependencies.
- Avoid direct dependencies between resources that can cause cycles.

6.7. Error: "Addressable asset not found in any group."

Problem Description:

This error occurs when Addressables cannot find a resource in any of the Addressables groups. Possible causes:

- The resource has been removed from the Addressables groups.

- The resource has not been correctly added to Addressables Groups.

- Incorrect resource address.

Decision:

1. **Check if the resource is available in Addressables Groups:**

   - Make sure that the resource is present in one of the groups in the window **Addressables Groups**.
   - If the resource has been moved or deleted, add it back in.

2. **Check the address of the resource:**

   - Make sure that the address used in the code exactly matches the address of the resource in Addressables Groups.
   - Check the case of the letters and the absence of extra spaces.

3. **Rebuild Addressables:**

   - After adding or modifying resources in Addressables Groups, be sure to perform the build **Addressables** through *Build > New Build > Default Build Script*.

Address verification example:

```
using UnityEngine;
using UnityEngine.AddressableAssets;

public class AddressCheckLoader : MonoBehaviour
{
    public string existingAddress;
    public string nonExistingAddress;

    void Start()
    {
        // Load an existing resource
        Addressables.LoadAssetAsync<GameObject>(existingAddress)
            .Completed += OnLoadDone;

        // Loading an existing resource (will throw an error)
        Addressables.LoadAssetAsync<GameObject>(nonExistingAddress)
            .Completed += OnLoadDone;
```

```
    }

  void OnLoadDone(UnityEngine.ResourceManagement.AsyncOperations
    .AsyncOperationHandle<GameObject> handle)
  {
    if (handle.Status == UnityEngine.ResourceManagement.AsyncOperations
    .AsyncOperationStatus.Succeeded)
    {
      Instantiate(handle.Result);
      Debug.Log("Resource loaded successfully.");
    }
    else
    {
      Debug.LogError("Resource not found.");
    }
  }
}
```

Additional recommendations:

- Use unique and descriptive addresses for resources.
- Regularly check that all required resources are available in Addressables Groups.

6.8. Error: "Build path not found or inaccessible."

Problem Description:

This error occurs when the specified path for an AssetBundles assembly is not available or does not exist. This may be due to incorrect Addressables profile settings or problems with directory permissions.

Decision:

1. **Check the profile settings Addressables:**

   - Go to *Window* > *Asset Management* > *Addressables* > *Groups*.
   - Click **Profile** and select **Manage Profiles**.
   - Ensure that the BuildPath and LoadPath variables point to existing and accessible directories.

2. **Make sure there are pathways in place:**

   - Check if the directories specified in the settings exist.
   - If not, create them manually or change the settings to existing paths.

3. **Check access rights:**

- Make sure that Unity has the necessary permissions to read and write to the specified directories.
- Especially relevant for paths located in protected system directories.

Example of a path check:

```
using UnityEditor;
using UnityEditor.AddressableAssets.Settings;
using UnityEngine;

public class PathChecker
{
    [MenuItem("Tools/Check Addressables Paths")]
    public static void CheckPaths()
    {
        AddressableAssetSettings settings = AddressableAssetSettingsDefaultObject.Settings;
        if (settings == null)
        {
            Debug.LogError("AddressableAssetSettings not found.");
            return;
        }

        string buildPath = settings.profileSettings.GetValueById(settings.activeProfileId,
"BuildPath");
        string loadPath = settings.profileSettings.GetValueById(settings.activeProfileId,
"LoadPath");

        if (!System.IO.Directory.Exists(buildPath))
        {
            Debug.LogError($"BuildPath does not exist: {buildPath}");
        }
        else
        {
            Debug.Log($"Build Path available: {build Path}");
        }

        if (!System.IO.Directory.Exists(loadPath))
        {
            Debug.LogError($"LoadPath does not exist: {loadPath}");
        }
        else
        {
            Debug.Log($"LoadPath available: {loadPath}");
        }
    }
}
```

Additional recommendations:
- Use relative paths instead of absolute paths to avoid project portability problems.
- Avoid using paths that require elevated write privileges.

6.9. Error: "Resource failed to load due to missing dependencies."

Problem Description:

This error indicates that the resource cannot be loaded because its dependencies are missing or have not been loaded. This can happen if Addressables failed to detect or correctly distribute dependencies between resources.

Decision:

1. **Check resource dependencies:**

   - Ensure that all required dependencies are present in Addressables Groups.
   - In Addressables Groups, check that the dependencies are distributed correctly and are in the correct groups.

2. **Rebuild Addressables:**

   - After adding or modifying dependencies, be sure to run the Addressables build via *Build > New Build > Default Build Script*.

3. **Use the dependency analysis tool:**

   - Addressables provides dependency analysis tools to help you identify missing or incorrect dependencies.

Example of dependency analysis:

```
using UnityEditor.AddressableAssets.Settings;
using UnityEditor.AddressableAssets;
using UnityEngine;

public class DependencyAnalyzer
{
  [MenuItem("Tools/Analyze Addressables Dependencies")]
  public static void AnalyzeDependencies()
  {
    AddressableAssetSettings settings = AddressableAssetSettingsDefaultObject.Settings;
    if (settings == null)
    {
      Debug.LogError("AddressableAssetSettings not found.");
      return;
    }
```

```
    foreach (var group in settings.groups)
    {
       foreach (var entry in group.entries)
       {
          var deps = settings.GetDependencies(entry, true);
          foreach (var dep in deps)
          {
             if (settings.FindAssetEntry(dep) == null)
             {
                Debug.LogError($"The resource '{entry.address}'
                       depends on a missing resource: '{dep}'");
             }
          }
       }
    }
    Debug.Log("Dependency analysis complete.");
  }
}
```

Additional recommendations:

- Use labels to group related resources and manage their dependencies.
- Regularly check and update dependencies when the project structure changes.

6.10. Error: "Catalog has expired."

Problem Description:

This error occurs when an application attempts to load resources from an obsolete Addressables directory. This can happen if the directory on the server has been updated, but the client part of the application has not updated its local directory.

Decision:

1. **Checking and updating the catalogue:**

   - Use the **CheckForCatalogUpdates** and **UpdateCatalogs** methods to check if updates are available and downloaded.

2. **Example of catalogue update:**

```
using UnityEngine;
using UnityEngine.AddressableAssets;
using UnityEngine.ResourceManagement.AsyncOperations;
using Cysharp.Threading.Tasks;
using System.Collections.Generic;
```

```csharp
public class CatalogUpdater : MonoBehaviour
{
    async void Start()
    {
        await UpdateCatalogIfNeeded();
    }

    public async UniTask UpdateCatalogIfNeeded()
    {
        try
        {
            var catalogUpdate = await Addressables.CheckForCatalogUpdates().Task;
            if (catalogUpdate.Count > 0)
            {
                await Addressables.UpdateCatalogs(catalogUpdate).Task;
                Debug.Log("Dependency analysis complete.");
            }
            else
            {
                Debug.Log("No catalog updates found.");
            }
        }
        catch (System.Exception ex)
        {
            Debug.LogError($"Error updating directory: {ex.Message}");
        }
    }
}
```

1. Handling errors during loading:

   - Implement mechanisms to retry downloads or notify the user when the application needs to be updated.

2. Catalogue version control:

   - Keep track of the catalogue versions and make sure that client applications are synchronised with the server versions.

Additional recommendations:

- Use a CDN or reliable servers to store the Addressables directory to minimise the chance of damage or loss of the directory.

- Regularly test catalogue updates on a variety of devices and network conditions.

6.11. Error: "Addressables.Release called too many times."

Problem Description:

This error occurs when the Addressables.Release method is called more times than required for a particular resource. This causes the resource to be prematurely unloaded, which can cause errors when trying to use it.

Decision:

1. Ensure that Release calls are properly accounted for:
   - For each call to LoadAssetAsync, there must be a corresponding call to Release.
   - Avoid multiple Release calls for the same resource without additional downloads.

2. Use a resource manager:
   - Implement a resource management system that tracks the number of downloads and uploads for each resource.

Example: Link counter for resources:

```
using UnityEngine;
using UnityEngine.AddressableAssets;
using UnityEngine.ResourceManagement.AsyncOperations;
using System.Collections.Generic;

public class ResourceManagerWithRefCount : MonoBehaviour
{
    private Dictionary<string, (AsyncOperationHandle<Object>, int)> resourceDictionary
        = new Dictionary<string, (AsyncOperationHandle<Object>, int)>();

    public void LoadResource(string address)
    {
        if (resourceDictionary.ContainsKey(address))
        {
            resourceDictionary[address] = (resourceDictionary[address].Item1,
resourceDictionary[address].Item2 + 1);
        }
        else
        {
            var handle = Addressables.LoadAssetAsync<Object>(address);
            resourceDictionary[address] = (handle, 1);
        }
    }

    public void ReleaseResource(string address)
    {
        if (resourceDictionary.ContainsKey(address))
        {
```

```
      var (handle, count) = resourceDictionary[address];
      if (count > 1)
      {
         resourceDictionary[address] = (handle, count - 1);
      }
      else
      {
         Addressables.Release(handle);
         resourceDictionary.Remove(address);
      }
   }
   else
   {
      Debug.LogWarning($"Attempt to unload a non-existent resource: {address}");
   }
}

void OnDestroy()
{
   foreach (var key in new List<string>(resourceDictionary.Keys))
   {
      Addressables.Release(resourceDictionary[key].Item1);
   }
   resourceDictionary.Clear();
}
}
```

Additional recommendations:
- Implement a single resource manager that will control the loading and unloading of resources, preventing redundant Release calls.
- Use weak links or tracking systems to automatically manage the lifecycle of resources.

6.12. Error: "Addressables cannot load asset from unloaded bundle."

Problem Description:

This error occurs when Addressables try to load a resource from an AssetBundle that has been unloaded or not loaded at all. This can happen if the AssetBundle dependency was unloaded before the resource was loaded.

Decision:

1. **Make sure all dependencies are loaded:**

   - Addressables automatically loads dependencies when you load the main resource, but make sure you don't unload AssetBundles until the load is complete.

2. **Avoid premature discharge:**

- Do not call Addressables.Release for AssetBundles or resources that are still in use.

3. **Use a dependency aware resource manager:**

- Implement a resource management system that tracks dependencies and ensures they are loaded before they are used.

Example of ensuring dependency loading:

```
using UnityEngine;
using UnityEngine.AddressableAssets;
using UnityEngine.ResourceManagement.AsyncOperations;
using Cysharp.Threading.Tasks;

public class DependencyAwareLoader : MonoBehaviour
{
    public string mainAssetAddress;

    async void Start()
    {
        try
        {
            // Load the main resource and its dependencies
            var handle = Addressables.LoadAssetAsync<GameObject>(mainAssetAddress);
            await handle.Task;

            if (handle.Status == AsyncOperationStatus.Succeeded)
            {
                Instantiate(handle.Result);
                Debug.Log("The main resource and its dependencies loaded successfully.");
            }
            else
            {
                Debug.LogError($"Failed to load the main asset at: {mainAssetAddress}");
            }
        }
        catch (System.Exception ex)
        {
            Debug.LogError($"Error loading resource: {ex.Message}");
        }
    }

    void OnDestroy()
    {
        // Unload the main resource, which will also unload its dependencies
        Addressables.Release(mainAssetAddress);
```

```
    }
}
```

Additional recommendations:
- Avoid manual dependency management by trusting the automatic management of Addressables.
- Regularly check and test resource loadings against their dependencies.

6.13. Error: "Addressables.ReleaseInstance called on non-instantiated object."

Problem Description:

This error occurs when the Addressables.ReleaseInstance method is called for an object that was not created via Addressables.InstantiateAsync. This causes errors because Addressables does not track such an object as a managed resource.

Decision:

1. **Use Addressables.InstantiateAsync to create the instances:**

   - Always use the Addressables.InstantiateAsync methods to create Addressable resource instances so that they are correctly tracked and managed by the Addressables system.

2. **Avoid calling ReleaseInstance for common objects:**

   - Call Addressables.ReleaseInstance only for objects created via Addressables.InstantiateAsync.

Example of correct usage:

```
using UnityEngine;
using UnityEngine.AddressableAssets;
using UnityEngine.ResourceManagement.AsyncOperations;

public class CorrectInstanceLoader : MonoBehaviour
{
    public string prefabAddress;
    private AsyncOperationHandle<GameObject> handle;
    private GameObject instance;

    void Start()
    {
        // Correct loading and instantiation of the object
        handle = Addressables.InstantiateAsync(prefabAddress, Vector3.zero,
Quaternion.identity);
        handle.Completed += OnInstanceLoaded;
    }
```

```
    void OnInstanceLoaded(AsyncOperationHandle<GameObject> handle)
    {
      if (handle.Status == AsyncOperationStatus.Succeeded)
      {
        instance = handle.Result;
        Debug.Log("Object instantiated successfully.");
      }
      else
      {
        Debug.LogError($"Failed to instantiate object at address: {prefabAddress}");
      }
    }

    void OnDestroy()
    {
      if (instance != null)
      {
        Addressables.ReleaseInstance(handle);
        Debug.Log("The instantiated object was successfully unloaded.");
      }
    }
}
```

Additional recommendations:
- Distinguish between objects created via Addressables and normal objects.
- Keep a clear record of the instances created so that they can be uploaded correctly.

6.14. Error: "Addressable system is disabled."

Problem Description:

This error occurs when the Addressables system is disabled or not configured in the project. This can happen if the Addressables package has been deleted or corrupted.

Decision:

1. **Check the installation of the Addressables package:**

   - Go to *Window > Package Manager*.
   - Make sure that the Addressables package is installed. If not, install it.

2. **Restore the settings Addressables:**

- Go to *Window > Asset Management > Addressables > Groups*.
- If Addressables are not initialised, they will be automatically initialised when the window is opened.
- If necessary, perform an Addressables build via *Build > New Build > Default Build Script*.

3. **Check the settings files Addressables:**

- Make sure that the AddressableAssetSettings.asset file is present in your project.
- If the file is corrupted or missing, restore it from a backup or recreate the Addressables settings.

Example of checking the Addressables setting:

```
using UnityEngine;
using UnityEngine.AddressableAssets;

public class AddressablesChecker : MonoBehaviour
{
  void Start()
  {
    if (AddressableAssetSettingsDefaultObject.Settings == null)
    {
      Debug.LogError("The Addressables system is not configured
        . Please install and configure Addressables.");
    }
    else
    {
      Debug.Log("The Addressables system is configured and ready to use.");
    }
  }
}
```

Additional recommendations:
- Regularly update the Addressables package to the latest stable version for new features and bug fixes.
- Avoid manually deleting Addressables files without using the Unity Package Manager.

6.15. Error: "Addressables cannot load asset because AssetBundle is not loaded."

Problem Description:

This error indicates that Addressables is attempting to load a resource from an AssetBundle that has not been loaded. This can happen if an AssetBundle dependency has been unloaded or has never been loaded.

Decision:

1. **Check the dependencies:**
   - Ensure that all dependent AssetBundles are loaded before loading the main resource.
   - Addressables automatically manage dependencies, but make sure you don't call Addressables.Release for dependencies before the download is complete.

2. **Rebuild Addressables:**
   - Ensure that all dependencies are correctly defined and included in the Addressables assembly.

3. **Use the correct loading methods:**
   - When loading resources, use methods that automatically load dependencies, such as LoadAssetAsync.

Example of correct loading of a resource with dependencies:

```
using UnityEngine;
using UnityEngine.AddressableAssets;
using UnityEngine.ResourceManagement.AsyncOperations;
using Cysharp.Threading.Tasks;

public class DependentAssetLoader : MonoBehaviour
{
  public string mainAssetAddress;

  async void Start()
  {
    try
    {
      // Load the main resource and its dependencies
      var handle = Addressables.LoadAssetAsync<GameObject>(mainAssetAddress);
      await handle.Task;

      if (handle.Status == AsyncOperationStatus.Succeeded)
      {
        Instantiate(handle.Result);
        Debug.Log("The main resource and its dependencies were loaded successfully.");
      }
    }
```

```
        else
        {
            Debug.LogError($"Failed to load the main asset at: {mainAssetAddress}");
        }
    }
    catch (System.Exception ex)
    {
        Debug.LogError($"Error loading resource: {ex.Message}");
    }
}

void OnDestroy()
{
    // Unload the main resource, which will also unload its dependencies
        if they are no longer in use
    Addressables.Release(mainAssetAddress);
}
}
```

Additional recommendations:
- Avoid manual management of dependencies by letting the Addressables system manage them automatically.
- Regularly check and test the loading of resources with their dependencies to prevent such errors.

6.16. General recommendations for avoiding errors

1. **Careful adjustment Addressables Groups:**

   - Organise groups in a logical and structured way to avoid confusion and errors when loading resources.

2. **Regular assembly Addressables:**

   - After making changes to resources or group settings, always perform an Addressables build to ensure that they work correctly.

3. **Use of logging:**

   - Implement a logging system to track resource loading and unloading to help identify and resolve issues quickly.

4. **Testing on different platforms and devices:**

   - Regularly test your project on target platforms and devices to detect and eliminate platform-dependent bugs.

5. **Study of documentation and communities:**

   - Check out the official Addressables documentation and participate in the developer communities to stay up to date on new features and solutions to common problems.

6. **Using the resource manager:**

   - Implement a resource manager that centrally manages the loading and unloading of resources, preventing redundant calls and memory leaks.

Conclusion of the section

In this section, we've covered the most common errors that developers may encounter when using Addressables in Unity, as well as methods for troubleshooting and preventing them. Understanding and addressing these issues in a timely manner will allow you to create more stable and efficient projects that take full advantage of the Addressables system. In the following sections, we will continue to explore additional aspects of working with Addressables, such as performance optimisation, version management and integration with other systems.

Section 7: Best Practices and Tips for Working with Addressables

Using Addressables in Unity provides many opportunities for efficient resource management, performance optimisation and flexible content loading. However, to maximise the potential of Addressables, it's important to follow some best practices and guidelines. In this section, we'll look at key approaches and tips to help you avoid common mistakes and create more manageable and productive projects.

7.1. Organisation of Addressables Groups

The organisation of Addressables groups plays an important role in managing resources and optimising their utilisation. The correct group structure allows you to efficiently allocate resources, manage dependencies and minimise load times.

Recommendations:

1. **Grouping by resource type:**

   - Create separate groups for different types of resources such as sprites, models, audio, scenes, etc..
   - This simplifies management and allows you to optimise the loading of specific resource types.

2. **Grouping by scene or level:**

   - For multi-level games, it is convenient to create groups corresponding to individual scenes or levels.
   - This allows the necessary resources to be loaded and unloaded along with the corresponding scene.

3. **Using labels:**

   - Use tags to group related resources to make them easier to find and download by category.
   - For example, the UI, Enemies, Environment tags can help you quickly access the resources you need.

4. **Minimising the number of groups:**

   - Avoid creating too many groups as this can complicate management and increase loading overheads.
   - Strive for a balance between logical organisation and performance.

Example of group structure:

```
- Images (Sprites)
- Models (3D models)
- Audio (Audio files)
- Scenes (Scenes)
- UI (Interface)
- Enemies (Enemies)
```

7.2. Correct naming of resources

Clear and descriptive naming of resources makes them easier to identify, locate and manage. This is especially important in large projects with many resources.

Recommendations:

1. **Use meaningful names:**

   - Names should clearly reflect the content or purpose of the resource.

   - For example, use Enemy_Goblin or UI_Button_Play instead of Prefab1.

2. **Avoid special characters and spaces:**

   - Use underscores (_) or hyphens (-) to separate words.

   - This will help avoid problems when loading resources and make it easier to work with the code.

3. **Follow a consistent naming style:**

   - Define a naming style (e.g. PascalCase, camelCase) and stick to it throughout the project.

   - This will improve the readability and consistency of the code.

4. **Add versions or prefixes as needed:**
   For resources that can be updated, add versions or prefixes such as, v1_, v2_.

An example of good naming:

- PlayerModel

- EnemyGoblin

- UI_Button_Play

- Scene_MainMenu

- Audio_BackgroundMusic

7.3. Using labels to organise resources

Labels allow you to group related resources independently of their Addressables groups. This makes it easier to filter and load resources by category.

Recommendations:

1. **Create tags for frequent categories:**

   - For example, the tags UI, Enemies, Environment, Animations.
   - This will allow you to quickly download all resources related to a particular category.

2. **Use multiple tags:**

   - A single resource can have multiple labels, providing flexibility in its categorisation.
   - For example, a sprite can have UI and Icons labels.

3. **Avoid excessive labelling:**

   - Try to use tags only for really necessary categories to avoid confusion and redundancy.

4. **Document the labels used:**

   - Keep a list of all the tags used and their purpose so the development team can quickly navigate around.

Example of how to use tags:

```
using UnityEngine;
using UnityEngine.AddressableAssets;
using UnityEngine.ResourceManagement.AsyncOperations;
using System.Collections.Generic;

public class LabelLoader : MonoBehaviour
{
    public string label = "UI";

    void Start()
    {
        // Load all resources labeled "UI"
        Addressables.LoadAssetsAsync<Object>(label, OnAssetLoaded)
            .Completed += OnLoadComplete;
    }

    void OnAssetLoaded(Object obj)
    {
        // Process the loaded object
        Debug.Log($"Loaded resource: {obj.name}");
    }
}
```

```
    void OnLoadComplete(AsyncOperationHandle<IList<Object>> handle)
  {
    if (handle.Status == AsyncOperationStatus.Succeeded)
    {
      Debug.Log("All resources with the label have been loaded successfully.");
    }
    else
    {
      Debug.LogError("Could not load resources with label.");
    }
  }
}
```

7.4. Optimising the size of AssetBundles

Minimising the size of AssetBundles helps reduce load times and memory consumption. Optimisation includes efficient compression, selecting the right formats and removing unnecessary resources.

Recommendations:

1. **Use appropriate compression techniques:**

   - **LZ4**: Fast decompression, suitable for resources that need to be loaded quickly.
   - **LZMA**: High compression rate, but slower in decompression, suitable for resources that are rarely loaded.

2. **Optimise textures:**

   - Use formats that are optimal for the target platforms (e.g. ETC2 for Android, PVRTC for iOS).
   - Reduce texture resolution where possible without losing quality.

3. **Remove unused resources:**

   - Regularly check Addressables groups and remove resources that are no longer used in the project.

4. **Use prefabs with generic materials:**

   - Common materials can be grouped into separate AssetBundles, reducing duplication and overall package size.

5. **Segment AssetBundles by functionality:**

   - Split AssetBundles into logical parts (e.g. interface, characters, environment) to load only the necessary packages depending on the scenario.

Compression setting example AssetBundles:

1. Open the window **Addressables Groups**: *Window > Asset Management > Addressables > Groups.*

2. Select the group you want to configure.

3. In the group inspector, find the **Build Settings** section.

4. Set **Compression** to LZ4 for resources that require fast loading or LZMA for resources that are rarely loaded.

5. Click **Apply** and run the Addressables build.

7.5. Dependency management

Dependency management between resources ensures that AssetBundles are loaded and unloaded correctly, preventing errors and conflicts.

Recommendations:

1. **Avoid cyclical dependencies:**

   - Structure the groups to avoid situations where AssetBundle A depends on AssetBundle B and AssetBundle B depends on AssetBundle A.

2. **Use generic AssetBundles for common dependencies:**

   - Create separate groups for common resources such as materials or shaders that are used in several other groups.

3. **Analyse dependencies regularly:**

   - Use the built-in Addressables tools to analyse and verify dependencies between resources.

4. **Minimise the number of dependencies:**

   - Try to reduce the number of dependencies between AssetBundles to reduce the complexity of managing them.

Example of dependency checking:

```
using UnityEditor.AddressableAssets.Settings;
using UnityEngine;

public class DependencyChecker
{
    [MenuItem("Tools/Check Addressables Dependencies")]
    public static void CheckDependencies()
    {
```

```
AddressableAssetSettings settings = AddressableAssetSettingsDefaultObject.Settings;
if (settings == null)
{
    Debug.LogError("AddressableAssetSettings not found.");
    return;
}

foreach (var group in settings.groups)
{
    foreach (var entry in group.entries)
    {
        var dependencies = settings.GetDependencies(entry, true);
        foreach (var dep in dependencies)
        {
            if (settings.FindAssetEntry(dep) == null)
            {
                Debug.LogError($"The resource '{entry.address}' depends
                    on a missing resource: '{dep}'");
            }
        }
    }
}
Debug.Log("Dependency analysis complete.");
}
}
```

7.6. Caching and memory management

Efficient cache and memory management helps to reduce device load and prevent application crashes.

Recommendations:

1. **Unload resources when they are no longer needed:**

    Use Addressables.Release or Addressables.ReleaseInstance to release memory occupied by resources.

2. **Use caching for frequently used resources:**

    Load resources into the cache to speed up their reloading and reduce network requests.

3. **Configure cache settings:**

    Set the maximum cache size and manage cache purging according to project requirements.

4. Monitor memory usage:

Use Unity Profiler to track memory usage and identify leaks.

7.7. Asynchronous loading and performance optimisation

Asynchronous loading allows resources to be loaded without blocking the main stream, providing a smooth and responsive user experience.

Recommendations:

1. Use asynchronous loading methods:

Prefer LoadAssetAsync, InstantiateAsync and other asynchronous Addressables methods for loading resources.

2. Use Task or UniTask to simplify asynchronous code:

This allows you to write cleaner and clearer asynchronous code without unnecessary colbacks.

3. Parallel loading of resources:

Load multiple resources at the same time to speed up the loading process.

4. Use preloading for frequently used resources:

Reboot resources that are likely to be needed in the near future to reduce latency when they are used.

7.8. Integrating Addressables with other systems

Addressables' integration with various systems and libraries extends its functionality and simplifies resource management in complex projects.

Recommendations:

1. Integration with Dependency Injection (DI) containers:

Use DI containers to manage dependencies and simplify testing.

2. Integration with analytics systems:

Track downloads and resource usage to analyse user behaviour and optimise content.

3. Integration with systems CI/CD:

Automate Addressables assembly and deployment processes with continuous integration and delivery systems.

Example of integration with a DI container (**Zenject**):

```
using Zenject;
using UnityEngine;
using UnityEngine.AddressableAssets;
using UnityEngine.ResourceManagement.AsyncOperations;
using Cysharp.Threading.Tasks;

public class AddressablesInstaller : MonoInstaller
{
    public override void InstallBindings()
    {
        Container.Bind<AddressableService>().AsSingle();
    }
}

public class AddressableService
{
    public async UniTask<GameObject> LoadGameObjectAsync(string address)
    {
        var handle = Addressables.LoadAssetAsync<GameObject>(address);
        await handle.Task;
        if (handle.Status == AsyncOperationStatus.Succeeded)
        {
            return handle.Result;
        }
        else
        {
            Debug.LogError($"Failed to load object at address: {address}");
            return null;
        }
    }

    public void ReleaseGameObject(GameObject obj)
    {
        Addressables.Release(obj);
    }
}

public class ExampleUsage : MonoBehaviour
{
    [Inject] private AddressableService _addressableService;
```

```
public string assetAddress;
private GameObject loadedObject;

async void Start()
{
  loadedObject = await _addressableService.LoadGameObjectAsync(assetAddress);
  if (loadedObject != null)
  {
    Instantiate(loadedObject, Vector3.zero, Quaternion.identity);
  }
}

void OnDestroy()
{
  if (loadedObject != null)
  {
    _addressableService.ReleaseGameObject(loadedObject);
  }
}}
```

7.9. Debugging and monitoring

Effective debugging and monitoring help identify and resolve resource utilisation issues, optimise memory usage and improve application stability.

Recommendations:

1. **Use Unity Profiler:**

   Track memory usage, resource load times, and other performance metrics.

2. **Enable detailed logging:**

   Log successful and unsuccessful resource load operations to simplify diagnostics.

3. **Use dependency analysis tools:**

   Check dependencies between resources and AssetBundles to prevent errors and optimise load times.

4. **Test on a variety of devices and platforms:**

   Ensure Addressables work correctly on all target platforms and devices.

Example of using logging for debugging:

```
using UnityEngine;
using UnityEngine.AddressableAssets;
using UnityEngine.ResourceManagement.AsyncOperations;

public class DebugLoader : MonoBehaviour
{
    public string assetAddress;

    void Start()
    {
        Addressables.LoadAssetAsync<GameObject>(assetAddress)
            .Completed += OnLoadDone;
    }

    void OnLoadDone(AsyncOperationHandle<GameObject> handle)
    {
        if (handle.Status == AsyncOperationStatus.Succeeded)
        {
            Instantiate(handle.Result);
            Debug.Log($"[DEBUG] Resource '{asset Address}' loaded successfully.");
        }
        else
        {
            Debug.LogError($"[DEBUG] Failed to load resource '{assetAddress}'
                . Status: {handle.Status}");
        }
    }

    void OnDestroy()
    {
        Addressables.Release(handle);
    }
}
```

7.10. Automation of assembly and deployment processes

Automating Addressables build and deployment processes increases development efficiency, reduces the likelihood of errors and speeds up the release process.

Recommendations:

1. **Use editorial scripts to automate:**

   - Create scripts that automatically collect Addressables, upload them to the server, and perform other necessary operations.

2. **Integrate with CI/CD systems:**

   - Set up continuous integration and delivery (e.g. using Jenkins, GitHub Actions, or GitLab CI) to automatically perform Addressables builds when code or resources change.

3. **Create piplines for deployment:**

   - Develop pipelines that automatically upload assembled AssetBundles to a server or CDN after a successful build.

An example of an editorial script for building and loading Addressables:

```
using UnityEditor;
using UnityEditor.AddressableAssets.Settings;
using UnityEngine;
using System.Diagnostics;

public class AutomatedAddressablesBuilder
{
  [MenuItem("Tools/Build and Upload Addressables")]
  public static void BuildAndUploadAddressables()
  {
    AddressableAssetSettings settings = AddressableAssetSettingsDefaultObject.Settings;
    if (settings == null)
    {
      UnityEngine.Debug.LogError("AddressableAssetSettings not found.");
      return;
    }

    // Build Addressables
    AddressableAssetSettings.BuildPlayerContent();
    UnityEngine.Debug.Log("Addressables were successfully collected.");

    // Upload to the server (example of using an external script)
    Process.Start("upload_script.bat");
    UnityEngine.Debug.Log("The server upload script has started.");
  }}
```

Explanation of the code:

- **BuildAndUploadAddressables()**:
  a. The Addressables assembly is performed first.
  b. An external script (upload_script.bat) is then run to upload AssetBundles to the server or CDN.

7.11. Version management and content updates

Version management and content updates keep resources up to date and provide users with access to new features and enhancements without having to update the entire application.

Recommendations:

1. **Use version metadata to AssetBundles:**

   Store AssetBundles version information to track changes and manage updates.

2. **Implement mechanisms to check for updates:**

   When you start the application, check for updates to the Addressables directory and download new versions of the resources.

3. **Use semantic versioning:**

   Apply semantic versioning to AssetBundles version control to ensure compatibility and clarity.

4. **Keep backups of older versions:**

   Store older versions of AssetBundles on the server to be able to roll back if necessary.

Example of checking and updating the catalogue:

```
using UnityEngine;
using UnityEngine.AddressableAssets;
using UnityEngine.ResourceManagement.AsyncOperations;
using Cysharp.Threading.Tasks;
using System.Collections.Generic;

public class CatalogVersionManager : MonoBehaviour
{
  async void Start()
  {
    await CheckAndUpdateCatalog();
  }

  public async UniTask CheckAndUpdateCatalog()
  {
```

```
    try
    {
        List<string> updates = await Addressables.CheckForCatalogUpdates().Task;
        if (updates.Count > 0)
        {
            await Addressables.UpdateCatalogs(updates).Task;
            Debug.Log("Addressables directory updated successfully.");
        }
        else
        {
            Debug.Log("No updates to Addressables directory found.");
        }
    }
    catch (System.Exception ex)
    {
        Debug.LogError($"Error checking or updating directory: {ex.Message}");
    }
  }
}
```

7.12. Security and management of access to resources

Securing and managing access to Addressables resources is especially important when resources are stored on remote servers or CDNs.

Recommendations:

1. **Use secure data transfer protocols:**

   Transmit AssetBundles and Addressables directories over secure protocols (e.g. HTTPS) to prevent data interception.

2. **Manage access rights to resources:**

   Restrict access to AssetBundles and Addressables directories to authorised users or applications only.

3. **Encrypt sensitive data:**

   If the resources contain sensitive data, consider encrypting them before uploading them to the server.

4. **Regularly update the server software:**

   Keep the server software on which resources are stored up to date to protect against vulnerabilities.

Example of using HTTPS to download Addressables:

1. **Configure the server to support HTTPS:**

   Make sure your server or CDN supports HTTPS and has a valid SSL certificate.

2. **Configure RemoteLoadPath using HTTPS:**

   In the Addressables profile, set RemoteLoadPath to a URL starting with https://.

7.13. Managing multiple downloads and requests

Efficient management of multiple downloads and requests prevents redundant network calls and saves device resources.

Recommendations:

1. **Use Singleton for the resource manager:**

   Create a single instance of the resource manager that will be responsible for uploading and downloading, preventing multiple downloads of the same resource.

2. **Check the status of the download before starting a new download:**

   Ensure that the resource is not already being downloaded before initiating a new download.

3. **Use caching for frequently used resources:**

   Store downloaded resources in a cache to reuse them without having to re-download them.

Example of preventing multiple downloads:

```csharp
using UnityEngine;
using UnityEngine.AddressableAssets;
using UnityEngine.ResourceManagement.AsyncOperations;
using Cysharp.Threading.Tasks;
using System.Collections.Generic;


public class ResourceManager : MonoBehaviour
{
    private static ResourceManager instance;
    public static ResourceManager Instance
    {
        get
        {
```

```csharp
        if (instance == null)
        {
            instance = FindObjectOfType<ResourceManager>();
            if (instance == null)
            {
                GameObject obj = new GameObject("ResourceManager");
                instance = obj.AddComponent<ResourceManager>();
            }
        }
        return instance;
    }
}

private Dictionary<string, AsyncOperationHandle<Object>> loadingHandles
    = new Dictionary<string, AsyncOperationHandle<Object>>();

public async UniTask<T> LoadResourceAsync<T>(string address) where T : Object
{
    if (loadingHandles.ContainsKey(address))
    {
        return loadingHandles[address].Result as T;
    }
    else
    {
        var handle = Addressables.LoadAssetAsync<T>(address);
        loadingHandles[address] = handle;
        await handle.Task;
        return handle.Result;
    }
}

public void ReleaseResource(string address)
{
    if (loadingHandles.ContainsKey(address))
    {
        Addressables.Release(loadingHandles[address]);
        loadingHandles.Remove(address);
    }
}
}
```

118

7.14. Documentation and training of the team

The well-documented Addressables system makes it easy to use and maintain, especially in team projects.

Recommendations:

1. **Create an Addressables guide for the team:**

    Describe group structure, naming rules, resource loading and unloading processes.

2. **Conduct regular trainings and knowledge sharing:**

    Train new team members on Addressables and share best practices.

3. **Enter detailed documentation of processes and scripts:**

    Describe the purpose and use of all scripts associated with Addressables.

4. **Use comments in the code:**

    Add explanatory comments to important parts of the code for easy understanding and support.

Example of a documentation section:

```
# Addressables Guide

## Group structure
- **Images**:  Contains all sprites and textures.
- **Models**: Contains 3D models and related materials.
- **Audio**:   Contains audio files.
- **Scenes**: Contains the scenes of the project.
- **UI**:  Contains user interface elements.

## Naming rules
- Use PascalCase for resource names.
- Prefixes for groups:
  - `Image_` for sprites.
  - `Model_` for 3D models.
  - `Audio_` for audio.
  - `Scene_` for scenes.
  - `UI_` interface elements.

## Loading and unloading processes
- All resource uploads must be done via `ResourceManager`.
- After use, resources must be released with `Addressables.Release`.

## Scripts
```

- **ResourceManager.cs**: Manages the loading and unloading of resources, preventing multiple downloads.
- **ImageManager.cs**: Controls the loading and displaying of images in the UI.

7.15. Monitoring and analytics

Implementing monitoring and analytics systems allows you to track resource usage, identify bottlenecks and optimise application performance.

Recommendations:

1. **Track successful and unsuccessful downloads:**

   Log resource load information for analysis and debugging.

2. **Use analytics systems:**

   Integrate Addressables with analytics systems (e.g. Unity Analytics) to track user behaviour and resource usage.

3. **Analyse performance data:**

   Use the data to optimise workload and resource management.

Example of integration with Unity Analytics:

```csharp
using UnityEngine;
using UnityEngine.AddressableAssets;
using UnityEngine.ResourceManagement.AsyncOperations;
using UnityEngine.Analytics;
using System.Collections.Generic;

public class AnalyticsLoader : MonoBehaviour
{
    public string assetAddress;

    void Start()
    {
        Addressables.LoadAssetAsync<GameObject>(assetAddress)
            .Completed += OnLoadDone;
    }

    void OnLoadDone(AsyncOperationHandle<GameObject> handle)
    {
```

```
    if (handle.Status == AsyncOperationStatus.Succeeded)
    {
        Instantiate(handle.Result);
        Debug.Log($"Resource '{asset Address}' loaded successfully.");
        // Send analytics event
        Analytics.CustomEvent("ResourceLoaded", new Dictionary<string, object>
        {
            { "Address", assetAddress },
            { "Timestamp", System.DateTime.UtcNow }
        });
    }
    else
    {
        Debug.LogError($"Failed to load resource '{assetAddress}'.");
        // Send an error event
        Analytics.CustomEvent("ResourceLoadFailed", new Dictionary<string, object>
        {
            { "Address", assetAddress },
            { "Timestamp", System.DateTime.UtcNow }
        });
    }
}

void OnDestroy()
{
    Addressables.Release(handle);
}
}
```

Conclusion of the section

In this section, we have discussed best practices and tips on how to effectively use the Addressables system in Unity. Following these tips will help you create more optimised, manageable, and productive projects, avoid common bugs, and keep your application or game stable. Remember that successful use of Addressables requires careful planning, regular testing, and continuous improvement of resource management approaches.

Section 8: Example

Let's look at a common example where we have startup data that should load on the first session and not change, until the next update. Such startup resources may include scene, prefabs, music, fonts, sprites. And also possible temporary resources in the form of shares or events, consisting of prefabs, atlases. These resources do not need to be stored and are dynamically loaded and unloaded.

Before you start, make sure your project has the **Addressables package** installed via the **Unity Package Manager**. Configure the **Addressables** system by creating a profile and setting the **Build Remote Catalog** options. All downloadable resources are added to their **Addressables** groups and we only need to write their implementations.

Brief plan:

1. The version of the catalogue is checked. If the version has not changed, the download is skipped.

2. When the catalogue version changes, a starter set of data (scene, sprites, music, fonts, prefabs) is loaded and stored in the cache.

3. Additional resources not stored in the cache are dynamically loaded.

4. Changing the version clears the old cache.

5. All downloads display progress in megabytes.

6. All steps are logged for debugging.

8.1: Initialising and checking the catalogue version

Create a script **AddressablesManager.cs:**

```
using System;
using System.Collections;
using UnityEngine;
using UnityEngine.AddressableAssets;
using UnityEngine.ResourceManagement.AsyncOperations;
using UnityEngine.ResourceManagement.ResourceLocations;

public class AddressablesManager : MonoBehaviour
{
    // Key for saving directory version
    private const string CatalogVersionKey = "CatalogVersion";

    // Saved version of the catalog
    private string cachedCatalogVersion;

    void Start()
```

```csharp
    {
        StartCoroutine(CheckCatalogVersion());
    }

    private IEnumerator CheckCatalogVersion()
    {

        Debug.Log("Initializing Addressables...");
        AsyncOperationHandle<string> catalogUpdateHandle =
            Addressables.CheckForCatalogUpdates();

        yield return catalogUpdateHandle;

        if (catalogUpdateHandle.Status == AsyncOperationStatus.Succeeded)
        {
            Debug.Log("Check completed. Catalog updates: "
                + catalog Update Handle.Result.Count);

            if (catalogUpdateHandle.Result.Count > 0)
            {
                Debug.Log("Directory updated. Loading...");
                StartCoroutine(UpdateCatalog());
            }
            else
            {
                Debug.Log("Directory is up to date. Loading resources from cache.");
                LoadCachedAssets();
            }
        }
        else
        {
            Debug.LogError("Error checking directory version.");
        }

        Addressables.Release(catalogUpdateHandle);
    }

    private IEnumerator UpdateCatalog()
    {

    }

}
```

124

8.2: Updating the catalogue and downloading the start data

Add the **UpdateCatalog** method to **AddressablesManager.cs**:

```csharp
private IEnumerator UpdateCatalog()
{
    // Update the directory
    AsyncOperationHandle catalogHandle = Addressables.UpdateCatalogs();

    yield return catalogHandle;

    if (catalogHandle.Status == AsyncOperationStatus.Succeeded)
    {
        Debug.Log("The directory was successfully updated. Clearing the old cache...");
        ClearCache();

        Debug.Log("Loading test data...");
        yield return LoadInitialAssets();
    }
    else
    {
        Debug.LogError("Error updating directory.");
    }

    Addressables.Release(catalogHandle);
}

private void ClearCache()
{
    Debug.Log("Clearing cache...");
    Caching.ClearCache();
    PlayerPrefs.DeleteKey(CatalogVersionKey);
    Debug.Log("Cache cleared.");
}

private IEnumerator LoadInitialAssets()
{
    string[] initialAssets = { "Scene_1", "SpritePack", "MusicTrack", "FontPack",
"PrefabPack" };
    foreach (var assetKey in initialAssets)
    {
        AsyncOperationHandle handle = Addressables.LoadAssetAsync<object>(assetKey);
        while (!handle.IsDone)
        {
            Debug.Log($"Loading {assetKey}: {handle.PercentComplete * 100:F2}%");
            yield return null;
```

```
        }

        if (handle.Status == AsyncOperationStatus.Succeeded)
        {
            Debug.Log($"{assetKey} loaded successfully.");
        }
        else
        {
            Debug.LogError($"Error loading {assetKey}.");
        }
        Addressables.Release(handle);
    }

    // Save the current directory version
    cachedCatalogVersion = Addressables.GetRemoteCatalogVersion();
    PlayerPrefs.SetString(CatalogVersionKey, cachedCatalogVersion);
    PlayerPrefs.Save();

    Debug.Log("All startup data loaded successfully.");
}
```

8.3: Loading resources from the cache

Add a method to load data from the cache:

```
private void LoadCachedAssets()
{
    Debug.Log("Loading test data from cache...");
    StartCoroutine(LoadInitialAssets());
}
```

8.4: Dynamic resource loading

Add a method for dynamic loading:

```
public void LoadDynamicAsset(string assetKey)
{
    StartCoroutine(LoadAssetAsync(assetKey));
}

private IEnumerator LoadAssetAsync(string assetKey)
```

```
{
    Debug.Log($"Dynamically loading resource: {assetKey}");
    AsyncOperationHandle handle = Addressables.LoadAssetAsync<object>(assetKey);

    while (!handle.IsDone)
    {
        Debug.Log($"Loading {assetKey}: {handle.PercentComplete * 100:F2}%");
        yield return null;
    }

    if (handle.Status == AsyncOperationStatus.Succeeded)
    {
        Debug.Log($"{assetKey} loaded successfully.");
    }
    else
    {
        Debug.LogError($"Error loading {assetKey}.");
    }

    Addressables.Release(handle);
}
```

8.5: Displaying download progress

Change the resource load cycle to show progress in megabytes:

```
private IEnumerator LoadInitialAssets()
{
    string[] initialAssets = { "Scene_1", "SpritePack", "MusicTrack", "FontPack",
"PrefabPack" };

    foreach (var assetKey in initialAssets)
    {
        AsyncOperationHandle<long> sizeHandle =
            Addressables.GetDownloadSizeAsync(assetKey);
        yield return sizeHandle;

        if (sizeHandle.Status == AsyncOperationStatus.Succeeded && sizeHandle.Result > 0)
        {
            Debug.Log($"Size of {asset Key}: {size Handle.Result / (1024 * 1024):F2} MB");
        }

        AsyncOperationHandle handle = Addressables.LoadAssetAsync<object>(assetKey);
        while (!handle.IsDone)
```

```
    {
      Debug.Log($"Loading {assetKey}: {handle.PercentComplete * 100:F2}%");
      yield return null;
    }

    if (handle.Status == AsyncOperationStatus.Succeeded)
    {
      Debug.Log($"{assetKey} loaded successfully.");
    }
    else
    {
      Debug.LogError($"Error loading {assetKey}.");
    }

    Addressables.Release(handle);
  }
}
```

Code Explanation:

1. **Directory initialisation:**

   The **CheckCatalogVersion** method checks if the catalogue is up-to-date. If required, an update is triggered.

2. **Clearing the cache:**

   The **ClearCache** method removes old data from the cache to free up space.

3. **Loading start-up data:**

   Start data is loaded when the catalogue is updated or from the cache if it is up to date.

4. **Dynamic loading:**

   The **LoadDynamicAsset** method allows you to load additional resources by key that are not stored in the cache.

5. **Download progress in megabytes:**

   Used **GetDownloadSizeAsync** to display the size of the data being downloaded.

8.6: Converting downloaded data into game objects

We've downloaded the data, now let's apply that data.

Complete **AddressablesManager.cs** with the following method:

```csharp
private IEnumerator ProcessLoadedAsset(string assetKey, object asset)
{
    Debug.Log($"Resource processing: {assetKey}");

    switch (asset)
    {
        case Sprite sprite:
            Debug.LogError($"Error loading {assetKey}.");
            CreateSpriteObject(sprite);
            break;

        case AudioClip audioClip:
            Debug.Log($"Playing audio from {assetKey}");
            PlayAudioClip(audioClip);
            break;

        case Font font:
            Debug.Log($"Using font from {assetKey}");
            ApplyFont(font);
            break;

        case GameObject prefab:
            Debug.Log($"Creating a prefab from {assetKey}");
            InstantiatePrefab(prefab);
            break;

        case string sceneName:
            Debug.Log($"Loading scene {assetKey}");
            yield return LoadSceneAsync(sceneName);
            break;

        default:
            Debug.LogWarning($"Unknown resource type: {assetKey}");
            break;
    }
}
```

8.7 Supporting methods

Now let's add methods for each resource type.

8.7.1 Sprite creation

```csharp
private void CreateSpriteObject(Sprite sprite)
{
    GameObject spriteObject = new GameObject(sprite.name);
    var spriteRenderer = spriteObject.AddComponent<SpriteRenderer>();
    spriteRenderer.sprite = sprite;

    // Position in the center of the scene
    spriteObject.transform.position = Vector3.zero;
    Debug.Log($"Sprite {sprite.name} was successfully added to the scene.");
}
```

8.7.2 Audio playback

```csharp
private void PlayAudioClip(AudioClip audioClip)
{
    GameObject audioObject = new GameObject("AudioSource_" + audioClip.name);
    var audioSource = audioObject.AddComponent<AudioSource>();
    audioSource.clip = audioClip;
    audioSource.loop = true;
    audioSource.playOnAwake = true;
    audioSource.Play();
    Debug.Log($"Audio track {audioClip.name} is playing.");
}
```

8.7.3 Application of the font

```csharp
private void ApplyFont(Font font)
{
    GameObject textObject = new GameObject("TextObject");
    var textMesh = textObject.AddComponent<TextMesh>();
    textMesh.font = font;
    textMesh.text = "Text example";
    textMesh.characterSize = 0.1f;

    // Place it above the sprite
    textObject.transform.position = new Vector3(0, 2, 0);
    Debug.Log($"Font {font.name} applied to text.");
}
```

8.7.4 Creating a prefab

```
private void InstantiatePrefab(GameObject prefab)
{
    GameObject instance = Instantiate(prefab);
    instance.name = prefab.name;

    // Place it in the center of the scene
    instance.transform.position = Vector3.zero;
    Debug.Log($"Prefab {prefab.name} created.");
}
```

8.7.5 Loading a scene

```
private IEnumerator LoadSceneAsync(string sceneName)
{
    AsyncOperation sceneLoad = UnityEngine.SceneManagement.SceneManager
        .LoadSceneAsync(sceneName);
    while (!sceneLoad.isDone)
    {
        Debug.Log($"Loading scene {scene Name}: {scene Load.progress * 100:F2}%");
        yield return null;
    }
    Debug.Log($"Scene {sceneName} loaded successfully.");
}
```

8.7.6 Introducing processing into resource loading

Now use the **ProcessLoadedAsset** method in the load process. Update the **LoadInitialAssets** method:

```
private IEnumerator LoadInitialAssets()
{

    string[] initialAssets = { "Scene_1", "SpritePack", "MusicTrack", "FontPack",
"PrefabPack" };

    foreach (var assetKey in initialAssets)
    {
        AsyncOperationHandle handle = Addressables.LoadAssetAsync<object>(assetKey);

        while (!handle.IsDone)
        {
            Debug.Log($"Scene {sceneName} loaded successfully.");
            yield return null;
        }
```

```
      if (handle.Status == AsyncOperationStatus.Succeeded)
      {
        Debug.Log($"{assetKey} loaded successfully. Processing...");
        yield return ProcessLoadedAsset(assetKey, handle.Result);
      }
      else
      {
        Debug.LogError($"Error loading {assetKey}.");
      }

      Addressables.Release(handle);
    }

    // Save the current directory version
    cachedCatalogVersion = Addressables.GetRemoteCatalogVersion();

    PlayerPrefs.SetString(CatalogVersionKey, cachedCatalogVersion);
    PlayerPrefs.Save();

    Debug.Log("All startup data has been successfully loaded and processed.");
}
```

8.7.7 Example of dynamic loading with processing

Update **LoadDynamicAsset** method:

```
public void LoadDynamicAsset(string assetKey)
{
    StartCoroutine(LoadAssetAsync(assetKey));
}

private IEnumerator LoadAssetAsync(string assetKey)
{
    Debug.Log($"Dynamically loading resource: {assetKey}");
    AsyncOperationHandle handle = Addressables.LoadAssetAsync<object>(assetKey);

    while (!handle.IsDone)
    {
        Debug.Log($"Loading {assetKey}: {handle.PercentComplete * 100:F2}%");
        yield return null;
    }

    if (handle.Status == AsyncOperationStatus.Succeeded)
    {
        Debug.Log($"{assetKey} loaded successfully. Processing...");
```

132

```
    yield return ProcessLoadedAsset(assetKey, handle.Result);
  }
  else
  {
    Debug.LogError($"Error loading {assetKey}.");
  }

  Addressables.Release(handle);
}
```

Conclusion

Loaded data is now handled based on its type, convert to game objects, audio, text or scenes. This architecture is scalable and you can add handlers for new data types. Logs and download progress will help you track the status of your downloads at all stages.

Section 9: Conclusion and advice

Throughout this book, we've taken an in-depth look at the Addressables system in Unity, its features, best practices, and how to solve common problems. Addressables provides powerful tools for resource management, performance optimisation, and flexible content loading, making it an indispensable tool for developers of various project sizes. In this final section we will summarise our findings, highlight key points and offer recommendations for future work.

9.1. Key findings

1. **Flexible resource management:** Addressables allows you to efficiently manage different types of resources (sprites, models, audio, scenes, etc.), ensuring that they are dynamically loaded and unloaded as needed.

2. **Performance optimisation:** Using Addressables helps to reduce load times, reduce RAM consumption, and improve the overall performance of an application or game.

3. **Asynchronous loading:** Addressables supports asynchronous resource loading, which allows you to create more responsive and smoother user interfaces without lags and freezes.

4. **Dependency management:** The system automatically manages dependencies between resources, simplifying the process of loading and unloading them, as well as preventing possible conflicts and errors.

5. **Dynamic content update:** Addressables allows you to update game content without having to release new versions of the app, which is especially useful for mobile and online platforms.

6. **Integration with other systems:** Addressables easily integrates with various tools and libraries such as Task, UniTask, analytics systems and CI/CD, extending its functionality and capabilities.

9.2. Recommendations for the effective use of Addressables

1. **Plan your Addressables structure in advance:** Well-organised Addressables groups will make it easier to manage and optimise resources. Separate resources by type, scene or other logical categories for better manageability.

2. **Use profiles for different platforms and environments:** Setting up separate profiles for development, testing and production allows you to flexibly manage the paths for loading and building resources, taking into account the specifics of each platform.

3. **Optimise the size of AssetBundles:** Split large AssetBundles into smaller ones corresponding to logical resource groups to reduce load times and memory usage.

4. **Implement a resource management system:** Implement a resource manager that centrally manages the loading and unloading of resources, preventing redundant calls and memory leaks.

5. **Rebuild Addressables on a regular basis:** After making changes to resources or group settings, always perform an Addressables build to ensure that the system is working correctly and error-free.

6. **Test on target devices:** Optimisation can vary greatly from device to device, so regular testing on target platforms can help identify and fix platform-dependent issues.

7. **Use profiling tools:** Unity Profiler and other tools can help you monitor memory usage, load times and other important metrics, allowing you to optimise your application's performance.

8. **Document your processes and settings:** Maintaining detailed documentation of Addressables settings and resource loading processes will facilitate project support and teamwork, especially when scaling up.

9. **Stay tuned for updates on Addressables:** Unity is constantly updating the Addressables system, adding new features and improvements. Regularly update the Addressables package to the latest stable version to take advantage of all the benefits and bug fixes.

10. **Learn from examples and communities:** Explore project examples and participate in developer communities to adopt best practices and resolve issues when working with Addressables.

9.3. Future prospects and development

The Addressables system continues to evolve with new features and enhancements to improve its efficiency and usability. In the future, you can expect integration with more advanced resource management tools, improved performance, and expanded dependency management and caching capabilities. Developers are encouraged to follow Unity updates and actively use the new Addressables features to create better and more optimised projects.

9.4. Additional resources

To further deepen your knowledge and master Addressables, it is recommended that you refer to the following resources:

1. **Official documentation Unity Addressables:** Unity Addressables Documentation

2. **Community Unity:** Unity Forums — an active developer community where you can find answers to questions and share experience.

3. **Tutorials and video tutorials:**

   - Unity Learn — free training materials and courses.
   - YouTube — many channels dedicated to Unity and Addressables.

4. **Books and articles:** Look for specialised books and articles on optimisation and resource management in Unity.

5. **GitHub and project examples:** Explore example projects on GitHub that use Addressables to solve real-world problems.

9.5. Final thoughts

Using Addressables in Unity is a powerful way to manage resources that can greatly improve the performance and flexibility of your project. Properly configuring and optimising Addressables can help you create more scalable and manageable applications and games, while providing a better user experience. I hope this book has provided you with all the knowledge and tools you need to use Addressables effectively in your projects.

Conclusion of the book

Unity's Addressables system opens up new opportunities for developers to efficiently manage resources, optimise performance and flexibly load content. In this book we have covered the main aspects of working with Addressables, from basic settings and resource loading, to advanced optimisation techniques and solving common errors.

Using the knowledge gained and following best practices, you will be able to maximise the use of Addressables in your projects, creating high quality and productive applications and games. Remember that successful development is a continuous process of learning and improvement, so don't stop exploring new features and applying best practices to your work.

I wish you success in developing and realising your ideas with Addressables in Unity!

Recommendations and advice

1. **Don't be afraid to experiment:** Try different Addressables group settings, resource loading and unloading methods to find the most effective solutions for your project.

2. **Keep an eye out for Unity updates:** New versions of Unity often contain improvements and new features for Addressables. Update Unity regularly and explore new features.

3. **Learn by doing:** Create small projects or try to implement individual Addressables functions to consolidate what you have learnt.

4. **Community feedback and support:** Participate in discussions on forums and social platforms, share your experiences and get advice from other developers.

5. **Automate processes:** Use editorial scripts and CI/CD systems to automate the build and deployment of Addressables to increase efficiency and reduce the risk of errors.

6. **Document your project:** Keep detailed documentation of how Addressables is used in your project, including group settings, profiles, and the process of uploading resources. This will make project support and teamwork easier.

7. **Monitor memory usage and performance:** Regularly profile your application or game, monitor memory usage and resource load times to identify and eliminate bottlenecks in a timely manner.

www.ingramcontent.com/pod-product-compliance
Lightning Source LLC
LaVergne TN
LVHW060123070326
832902LV00019B/3103